CALLED
TO SUFFER
CALLED
TO TRIUMPH

Eighteen True Stories by Persecuted Christians

CALLED TO SUFFER CALLED TO TRIUMPH

Herbert Schlossberg

Forward by Brother Andrew of Open Doors

MULTNOMAH

Multnomah Press
Portland, Oregon

Edited by Al Janssen and Steve Halliday
Cover design by Durand Demlow

CALLED TO SUFFER, CALLED TO TRIUMPH
© 1990 by Herbert Schlossberg
Published by Multnomah Press
10209 SE Division Street
Portland, Oregon 97266

Multnomah Press is a ministry of Multnomah School of the Bible, 8435 NE Glisan Street, Portland, Oregon 97220.

Printed in the United States of America.

Library of Congress Cataloging-in-Publication Data

Schlossberg, Herbert.
    Called to suffer / Herbert Schlossberg.
      p. cm.
    ISBN 0-88070-409-8 (pbk.)
    1. Christian martyrs—Biography. 2. Christian martyrs—Communist countries—Biography. 3. Persecution—History—20th century. 4. Persecution—Communist countries—History—20th century. 5. Communist countries—Church history. I. Title.
BR1608.5.S35   1990
272'.9—dc20   90-46290
                               CIP

90 91 92 93 94 95 96 97 98 99 - 10 9 8 7 6 5 4 3 2 1

ACKNOWLEDGMENTS

*The author and publisher express their appreciation
to the following groups for making it possible
for us to collect the experiences
of the contributors to this book:*

*Open Doors with Brother Andrew
The Fieldstead Institute
Central European Mission Fellowship
International Teams
Chinese Church Research Center*

CONTENTS

Foreword 9
Introduction 11

Asia

1. Faith After Tiananmen (China) 25
2. Acts, Chapter 29 (China) 41
3. Lessons in Longsuffering (China) 53
4. Life Out of Ashes (India) 61
5. Spiritual Warfare in Kathmandu (Nepal) 77
6. When Christianity and Hinduism Collide (Nepal) 83
7. Alone in an Islamic Sea (Afghanistan) 95

Middle East and Africa

8. Study the Bible, Go to Jail (Egypt) 105
9. Standing Up to the Yad L'Achim (Israel) 119
10. Islam Makes a "Big Catch" (Nigeria) 129

Latin America

11. The Carrot and the Stick (Cuba) 139
12. Uncertainties Under Castro (Cuba) 145
13. Repression with a "Human Face" (Nicaragua) 155

Eastern Europe

14. A Traffic Accident, Romanian Style (Romania) 167
15. Vanya Meets the KGB (USSR) 175
16. Standing Strong Despite Opposition (Hungary) 193
17. The File (Czechoslovakia) 203
18. The Pastor and the Committee (Bulgaria) 217

Epilogue 233

FOREWORD

Several years ago I was in Budapest, Hungary, visiting one of the leading pastors of that city. As I sat there with about a dozen other pastors and elders, the door opened and in walked an old friend, a pastor from Romania. It was a pleasure for all of us to see him, for he had been in prison on my previous trip to his country.

This pastor sat in the group with us and looked at me expectantly, as if I were about to speak. But I was quiet too. I had been speaking to the group, but I knew it was time to stop. When you are in the presence of someone who has paid a price for his faith, you want to be silent and learn, because you know that some day you may be called upon to do the same.

Finally this Romanian brother broke the silence. "Andrew, are there any pastors in prison in Holland?"

"No," I replied.

"Why not?"

I thought for a moment and finally said, "I think it must be because we do not take advantage of all the opportunities God gives us."

Then came the most difficult question. "Andrew, what do you do with 2 Timothy 3:12?"

I opened my Bible and turned the pages while all the church leaders looked on expectantly. Then I read out loud, "All who desire to live a godly life in Christ Jesus will be persecuted."

Slowly, I closed the Bible and said to him, "Brother, please forgive me. We do nothing with that verse."

Until Jesus comes there will always be a suffering Church. If we don't use our God-given opportunities to help those suffering for their faith in Christ, I believe we can expect persecution to come to us in the free world.

We are called to change the world so that every Christian has enough liberty to worship according to the Bible. We don't deserve our freedom. We have it by God's grace for a purpose—to care for and strengthen other members of the Body of Christ who are suffering.

This book will help you fulfill that purpose. These stories of your brothers and sisters who have paid the price and made it through victoriously are testimony to the fact that we can make a difference.

Listen to them carefully as you read. Learn from them. Then rise up to help them and millions more like them. The day may come when you'll have to pay the price they did. But, be encouraged. On that day you can expect their help in return.

Brother Andrew
Ermelo, Holland
July, 1990

INTRODUCTION

I fidget uneasily in a hotel room in a large Chinese city, trying to pass the time with a book. The dreary day has gone by slowly, made drearier still by the depressing industrial setting that spreads out before my window at the back of the hotel. The shadows first lengthen, then slowly disappear as the night closes in, and still I wait. A little after 9 P.M. there is a knock at the door. I swing the door open cautiously, and my guide enters. She is an expatriate Chinese who tells me that she has completed the arrangements for our planned excursion. She easily blends in with the local population, much more easily than I will. Hurriedly and softly, she explains what we are about to do. I put on my coat, and we walk out of the room, proceed down the corridor to the elevator, and enter the street.

After a time we reach an alley off a side street and stop in a dark place as she pulls out of her purse one of the surgical-type white masks that the Chinese wear to protect themselves from the winter cold. I slip it on and, Caucasian features hidden, follow the lead of my guide as she navigates her way in a circuitous path I would never be able to retrace. The frequent turns give us opportunities to glance around and check for anyone who might be following. It's late enough that the streets are nearly deserted, making us more conspicuous than we would like. As we cut through back alleys and courtyards, I think ruefully of the amateurish disguise that would withstand only the most cursory of examinations. I'm too tall to pass easily for a Chinese, and my clothing is obviously foreign.

As we pass through one of the alleys my guide grips my arm and pulls me to a doorway which looks like all the others we have passed. Without knocking, she opens the door and pushes me through. The first thing I see is the anxious face of a Chinese man of about forty. His eyes look worried, but he welcomes me with a smile and a handshake and invites me with a gesture to sit down.

As I take the chair I glance around quickly. We're in a small room dominated by a bed pushed up against one of the walls. There is an old table, a few battered chairs, clothing hanging from pegs on a wall, a bicycle leaning against another wall, all of it badly lit by a small bulb hanging from the ceiling. Our host serves us tea and biscuits from a hot plate on a sideboard, but wastes little time in small talk. He speaks quietly and hurriedly, the translator breaking in every couple of sentences to tell me what he is saying. I write as fast as I can on the legal pad, straining to see in the dim light and grateful for the breaks in her monologue when the English stops and the Chinese begins. After ten minutes, my ballpoint runs out of ink, but the guide quickly pulls a pen out of her purse, and I'm back in business.

Our Chinese Christian friend is part of a house church, which is to say he worships illegally. His story includes a father imprisoned unjustly and then murdered by the regime, and his own lifetime is filled with discrimination of various kinds. After an hour of conversation his mother comes in, a bright and smiling woman whose cheerful countenance differs markedly from her son's somberness and which belies her many years of suffering. Later, a nephew and niece enter to see the visitors from overseas. Finally, tablet crammed with barely legible writing, we rise and say our goodbyes. On the way to the hotel our step is lighter, and I even remove the mask and am relieved by the freshness of the cold night air.

Much of the material in this book was gathered in similar ways, some of it by the author, some by traveling staff members of Open Doors with Brother Andrew, some of it by mission workers with other organizations. Sometimes we used tape recorders. In other cases our friends thought it would be too dangerous to have their voices taped, and we relied on hastily scrawled notes as interviewer, informant, and sometimes interpreter struggled together to provide a coherent and true story for Christians living in freedom. Our interview might be conducted in a small-town Hungarian parsonage, an Indian hotel, a church office in Bucharest, a back yard in Kathmandu, a manufacturing company in Tiberias, an apartment in Moscow. In one case a manuscript was taken out of a communist country by an unofficial conduit.

These stories feature great diversity. Representatives of a local Hindu establishment in India, enraged at the successes of a Christian ministry, beat up and rob a pastor and his wife and rape a young woman who lives with them. A Romanian pastor survives an attempt on his life. He ends up with a crippled arm after his car is rammed deliberately by a bus driver acting on orders of the state intelligence service. A Nepalese Christian accused of preaching Christ languishes with criminals in a crowded, filthy holding cell, and learns that his pregnant wife is also in jail. A Chinese pastor is thrown into prison for refusing to put himself under the authority of the puppet organization the state set up to facilitate its hold over the churches. He emerges twenty-one years later, and his family doesn't recognize him. Communist teachers in a small Hungarian village do all they can to disrupt the lives of Christian children. Two visitors from Morocco disappear into an Egyptian prison, punished for the crime of attending Bible studies. Six months and numerous beatings later they are expelled from the country after an international campaign has been mounted on their behalf.

But we have here something much more than "cases." These are the life stories of flesh-and-blood people, some of which are told to us at the cost of fearful risks to the safety of the tellers should the authorities learn their identities.

We need to put these personal memoirs in their proper context. The violations of religious liberty related here do not stand alone, but are part of a larger pattern of injustices. A society that jails a Christian because he has converted from Hinduism invariably will do other things that are unjust. This is quite apart from the fact that all societies, no less than all people, are imperfect. But the imperfections of, say, Czechoslovakia are not to be spoken of in the same breath as those of Italy. The Italians have much they might wish were different, but those who hold unpopular religious and political views are not languishing in fake psychiatric wards that are little more than torture chambers.

It's important to place religious persecution in the larger context in order to help us avoid over emphasizing its uniqueness and then romanticizing it. People who grow rhapsodic about the "purity" of the persecuted church are not likely to have seen much of it. If we look closely at Christians living in the countries of persecution, we can recognize that they are not too different from us, although their circumstances may be such as we can hardly imagine. That is, they show a confusing combination of saintliness and sin, courage and fear, wisdom and foolishness—just as we ought to expect.

But if we resist the temptation to make too much of these situations, let us not make the opposite mistake. If we don't romanticize persecution, let us also not trivialize it. There is something unique about punishing an innocent person for what he believes about God and how he puts that belief into action. Even if we have no personal experience with this we should not be blinded to the biblical teaching that persecution is normal and to be expected.

There was a time in the memory of people still living in the countries represented in this book when Christians were not persecuted for their faith. Persecution came where it did not exist earlier, and that is why we in other lands must not become complacent. Their world is not our world, but ours could become much like theirs. Persecution has been a part of the Christian experience from the beginning. In fact, we should consider the sufferings of the prophets of Israel as part of the same process:

> Some faced jeers and flogging, while still others were chained and put in prison. They were stoned; they were sawed in two; they were put to death by the sword. They went about in sheepskins and goatskins, destitute, persecuted and mistreated—the world was not worthy of them. They wandered in deserts and mountains, and in caves and holes in the ground (Hebrews 11:36-38).

And Jesus warned his followers to expect the same: "Remember the words I spoke to you: 'No servant is greater than his master.' If they persecuted me, they will persecute you also" (John 15:20).

It would be foolish in the extreme for those of us who practice our faith without fear to take our freedom for granted and ignore the experience of our predecessors and many of our contemporaries. On occasions too numerous to tally, a part of the Christian church enjoying peace and security has fallen on hard times from persecutors; seldom has it taken the trouble to learn beforehand how other churches have coped with such circumstances. A wealth of usable knowledge has been won at great cost by those who suffer before we do, and it is only sensible to expend some effort to make use of it.

I recently ran across one homely example that illustrates the point. A few years ago the Christian poet Irina Ratushinskaya found herself jammed into a *Stolypin* railroad car full of prisoners being shipped to a Soviet labor camp. She ate the piece of bread she was handed, but put the salted herring in her pocket for later. As the journey continued the prisoners around her were tormented by thirst, much intensified by eating the herring. As she expected, the guards ignored their pleas for water. Later, at the transit prison where there was plenty of water, she retrieved the herring from her pocket and ate it. How did she know what to expect? She had read it in a bootlegged copy (probably typewritten *samizdat*) of Alexander Solzhenitsyn's book *The Gulag Archipelago*. She comments on the usefulness of her predecessor's example:

> Thank you, Alexander Solzhenitsyn, for your priceless counsels! Who can say whether Igor and I would have had the presence of mind to burn all letters and addresses while the KGB hammered on our doors, had we not read your works? Or would I have been able to summon sufficient control not to bat an eyelid when they stripped me naked in prison? Without you, would I have grasped that cardinal principle for all prisoners of conscience: "Never believe them, never fear them, never ask them for anything."? [1]

Christians who suffer for their faith go through an enormous range of experiences, from the mildest to the most severe. There is not one persecution, but many. In making this point it's worth noting that we have deliberately used the term differently than did some of our informants. Not too long ago I was sitting with two friends in the living room of a pastor in Czechoslovakia. We were enjoying a lively conversation with the pastor and his wife and grown son. When I spoke of those who persecute Christians, the pastor interrupted and exclaimed: "We are not persecuted here. We are just under pressure." He explained that they understood persecution to mean beatings, imprisonment, and being put to death (all of which had in fact been part of the Czechoslovakian experience in the four decades or so since the Communists had taken over). The reader can judge for himself whether the Czechoslovak author in this book describes a situation which ought to be termed "persecution."

It's interesting to ponder that the Czech pastor who told us Christians were not persecuted had carefully instructed us to come at night, to exit our taxi some distance from his place, and to turn into his entrance only when nobody was in sight. After he welcomed us into his house he removed the telephone from the table on which it was placed, put it in the foyer behind him, covered it with cushions, and closed the door. When it was time for us to depart, he turned out the light in the hallway, walked outside to make sure the coast was clear, and only then signaled us to follow him into the dark street. But he didn't consider that what they were enduring should be called "persecution."

This differing use of terminology is trivial compared with disputes concerning why Christians end up in jail or labor camps or suffer other disabilities. Whom shall we believe concerning the reason Christians are punished by the law? Some countries with the worst record of persecuting Christians point to provisions in their constitutions for the complete separation of church and state and the freedom of religious belief. This is their answer to accusations based on long lists of believers in jail cells, work camps, and internal exile, as well as more subtle means of punishment.

Soviet officials, for example, have insisted (until very recently) that all those victims of persecution were really guilty of criminal offenses. Now, there is a sense in which that is true. When it is against the law to give religious instruction to young people, to minister to those with physical needs, to speak of Christ outside of the four walls of the registered church building, to print Bibles and other literature or to import them from outside the country, then Christians who believe they have a duty before God to do these things are transformed by unjust laws and court procedures into criminals. The regime may be accurate in saying that Christians are free to believe as they wish as long as their external actions do not follow suit, but that kind of religion has only a slight and misleading resemblance to Christianity.

It has to do rather with a false idea of the faith that is, in some settings, as common within the church as outside it. Sometimes this view is called pietism, in that it concentrates its attention on the inner spiritual life while treating as relatively unimportant external actions and relationships. Thus the believer prays, reads the Scriptures (if they happen to be available, as they often are not in countries where governments put all the emphasis on this inner kind of freedom to believe), and practices personal ethical values. Both the repressive regime and pietist Christianity can live with that kind of religion. If believers confined themselves to it, they would have far less difficulty with their rulers. But the Christians who tell their stories in this book know that this arrangement is entirely unsatisfactory.

With regularity, the Old and New Testaments both affirm that the inner life of piety, of worship of the living God, is connected with the outward performance of acts of worship and of mercy. "Learn to do right! Seek justice, encourage the oppressed. Defend the cause of the fatherless, plead the case of the widow" (Isaiah 1:17). "Do not merely listen to the word, and so deceive yourselves. Do what it says" (James 1:22). The New Testament vision of the church considers the propagation of the gospel to be so important that the final words of Jesus before his ascension were ". . . go and make disciples of all nations, baptizing them in the name of the Father and of the Son and of the Holy Spirit, and teaching them to obey everything I have commanded you" (Matthew 28:19f). This vision of the life of the follower of Christ is very far from the docile, privatized existence that totalitarian regimes are willing to live with.

But even that kind of deformed Christianity is too much for some of the enemies of Christ. They refuse to allow any version of Christian faith, no matter how truncated. At times this mentality dominated the Soviet and Chinese Communist regimes, and the church seemed to be on its way to extinction. Albania has made all forms of religious expression illegal and has harshly suppressed even private house ceremonies. Uncounted millions of Christians in such countries have been murdered in just a few short decades. And in some Moslem countries no externally observable expression of Christian faith is permitted—not so much as a cross—except perhaps for foreigners residing in the country.

In at least one predominantly Moslem country with ancient Jewish and Christian communities, an ominous threat is uttered when people feel provoked: "Soon we're going to start on Saturday and finish on Sunday." This means that when conditions permit, they'll eradicate the Jews (Saturday) and then the Christians (Sunday). This threat has now surfaced in Israel where Arab Christians suspected of only lukewarm support for the uprisings have been given the same message. Often people uttering such threats in Israel have also demanded that Christians remove crosses from their clothing.

These private threats suggest forms of persecution that we have not yet considered. Persecution does not come only from the government. It often comes from neighbors, co-workers, teachers, even family members. In fact, the government may be the best source of justice for Christians who otherwise would suffer greatly from other groups. At least one excellent example of such a situation is found in this book. There may be a strange paradox in that a government that persecutes in one context will protect in another. Sometimes these contradictions seem inexplicable. But other times the government may be changing its policies temporarily to serve foreign policy needs. Or local officials may choose to enforce the law selectively so that believers may be treated differently than others in the neighboring town or province, or differently than they themselves were treated the previous month.

It should not surprise us that such conditions change in this spotty way, for that is how most historical circumstances change. And the history of persecution confirms this sort of variability. The Book of Acts shows persecutions arising, then cooling off, and then coming to life again. That continued throughout most of the life of imperial Rome.

The importance for us of these first-hand accounts does not lie in the way they represent what is currently happening. Although they are all recent, conditions will certainly change. In fact, in the east European countries they have already changed. But a persecution that ebbs in one place will mount in another (or in the same place a little later). A persecution may change its character in, say, China, but we may be sure that some aspects of the Chinese situation will reappear elsewhere. The advantage of a book such as this with its variety of experiences is that it shows us in the words of those who are undergoing persecution what it means to suffer for Christ. And it helps the rest of us to become mentally and spiritually prepared for the same conditions in our own country.

The faith chapter of the letter to the Hebrews (quoted earlier) which so dramatically tells of the persecution of the Old Testament saints, is followed immediately by a chapter which tells of the role that suffering plays in the Christian's experience. It begins by showing that Christ is the true exemplar in this area as in every other. "Let us fix our eyes on Jesus," it says, "the author and perfecter of our faith, who for the joy set before him endured the cross, scorning its shame, and sat down at the right hand of the throne of God. Consider him who endured such opposition from sinful men, so that you will not grow weary and lose heart" (Hebrews 12:2-3).

The passage goes on to speak of suffering as a discipline which leads to the same kind of blessing that a father's discipline does for his children. That is a lesson that few children understand until they are grown. And it is usually from the elderly who have gone through much persecution that we hear their experiences related to such passages.

With only two exceptions our writers are all still living in the countries of their suffering; these are not *émigré* stories. Most of the chapters in this book come from personal interviews. The following names are pseudonyms:

Jiang Shipu, Kwan Ying, Li Wan, Ayub Zahir, Aljabar Burani, Renaldo Perez, José Fuentes, John Bent, Irina Andreevna Pogodina, Tibor Lanyi, Maria Cerny.

Notes

1. Irina Ratushinskaya, *Grey Is the Color of Hope*, translated by Alyona Kojevnikov (New York: Alfred A. Knopf, 1988), p. 10. Another Russian Orthodox woman cited the same principle of detachment that she also learned from Solzhenitsyn, explaining how it stood her in good stead as the Soviet secret police questioned her. Tatiana Goricheva, *Talking About God Is Dangerous: The Diary of a Russian Dissident*, translated from the German by John Bowden (New York: Crossroad, 1987), p. 5.

ASIA

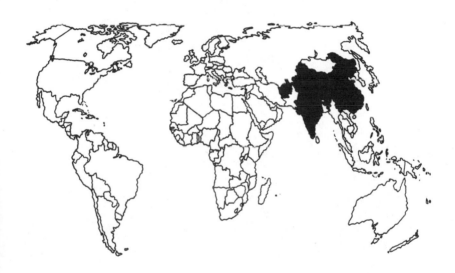

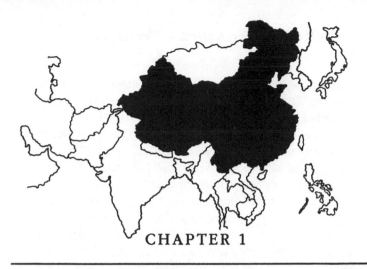

CHAPTER 1

FAITH AFTER TIANANMEN
by Jiang Shipu

*Introduction: The modern history of the
church in China seems to provide one miracle
after another. By the time the Cultural
Revolution ended in 1976 the church was
thought to have virtually disappeared. Instead it
emerged, as from a shell, and showed that
during the years underground it had multiplied
many times over.*

*But the church was largely a movement of the
poor and uneducated. Nobody in a position of
authority could profess Christian faith and keep
his job. Christians willing to speak up could not
easily gain a hearing from the educated classes.
This situation was dramatically overturned in
June 1989 when a panicky national leadership,
unable to cope with the burgeoning pro-
democracy movement, ordered the army to clear*

the demonstrators from Tiananmen Square in Beijing. The result was the infamous massacre.

And this led to another surprise. The intellectuals, whose disaffection from the regime had gone largely unexpressed, were either enraged or sickened by the mass bloodshed. More than that, there was mass disillusionment. For thousands who had borne so patiently the countless disappointments, the broken promises, the living in fear, the economic futility, this was the last straw. Now able to see clearly the evil of the ideology that had gripped their country for forty years, they were cast adrift with nothing else to hope in.

As this is written, it is a year since the massacre, and we have reports of thousands of intellectuals turning to Christ. In at least five university cities no less than ten percent of the students have been reported as turning to Christianity. In a way this is even more amazing than the revival during the Cultural Revolution. For the revolution that was led by intellectuals is now being deserted by those who made it.

Along with the revival has come a fresh crackdown by the authorities against the church, especially the house churches. Although not as serious as was at first feared after the massacre, it is bringing new hardships to the church. Roman Catholics in particular are suffering greatly, as the regime continues to give preference to both Protestants and Catholics who stick to the state-promoted church organizations.

Jiang Shipu is one of these new Christian intellectuals, and we are fortunate to have his story so soon after the events he reports.

• • •

I was born in 1969, but by the time I was eighteen I felt the way an old man must feel. Such was the tension and physical strain that came from the examination schedule at Beida University. Not everyone was affected as I was, but from a child my parents had drilled into me the idea that passing exams and getting into the university were the most important things in life. The pressures were made bearable only because the other children in my school were suffering in the same way.

The difficulty of such an upbringing was made somewhat easier by two advantages. The first is that I had a natural ability to do academic work and I could handle the courses in both humanities and science. Second, I was attending one of the finest schools in the country—the number one high school in Harbin. I only got into it because my father, a high-ranking army officer, was able to pull strings. I never felt any guilt about this because all my classmates had been able to enter for the same reason. It was accepted as normal. One disadvantage, however, was that my father never let me forget what he had done for me. He would always say, "I put my career on the line to get you there. If you fail to get into the university, I'll be disgraced."

Thus, when I came to the most important three days of my life in July 1987—the university entrance exams—the pressure on me was far greater than an outsider could imagine. For perhaps the first time since I had begun school I reflected on this question: "Does my life's happiness really depend on whether I obtain a certain grade on an exam? If I get one grade lower than the one that is required, is my life a ruin?" In China, the answer is yes. Getting into the university is a passport to prestige and comfort. It does not guarantee success, but in a society where the business of sheer physical survival is never far from anyone's mind, it gives a critical advantage. The best placements our society has to offer go to university graduates, and to no one else.

To the great relief of my family, I was not one of the

six million students that year who considered their life a
ruin. I was one of the five percent who won a place at a
university. I was able to study philosophy at the best
university in Beijing (some would say in all of
China)—Beida University.

I chose philosophy because I preferred it to science.
As I try to think why that was so, I recall an experience
in junior high school. Our science teacher was showing
us how animals move and used a small fish in a tank as
an illustration. As we watched it swim in the tank, the
teacher asked, "Can any of you tell me what would
happen if we cut off one of its fins?" There was a chorus
of opinion. Then she picked up the fish and snipped off
the top fin. We watched it struggle. "What would happen
if we cut off another fin?" And she snipped again. Finally,
the fish had no fins at all and just sank to the bottom of
the tank, its mouth gaping helplessly, and its eyes staring
at us accusingly—or so I thought. Many times I was to
feel like that fish, shorn by God of all my self-protection
and allowed to sink to the bottom where he rescued me.

But that is to jump ahead. For now, as a new student
at Beida University embarked on the study of
philosophy, I felt on top of the world. I was a winner,
one of the elite destined for fame and fortune. Or so I
thought.

I can see in retrospect that my mind was not well
developed. The Chinese educational system does not
encourage questioning or depth of thought. Rather, the
student obediently memorizes whatever his instructors
tell him. I had no religious consciousness to speak of. I
was a Communist of sorts, having grown up in a family
and society that taught only that set of beliefs. Typical of
my generation, I accepted them without question. We
didn't choose communism; it was simply ingrained into
us, and we absorbed it. At school I joined the Communist
Youth League, again without giving it any thought,
knowing that it was necessary to get into the university.
It was common knowledge what the authorities

considered the "Three Goods" for admission: good health, good grades, and good politics.

I arrived in Beijing the autumn of 1987 and began university life. On the whole conditions were tough. I shared a dorm with seven others. We were always hungry, taking our tin plates to the mess hall three times a day, receiving a dollop of rice and some greens, and going outside to squat on the grass to eat it as there was no room inside. We were always cold in the winter, since the dorms had no heat.

The academic facilities were poor also, even at China's premier university. We would draw lots to see who would get to sit in the library. Previous winners could not draw again. Any student would be lucky to get into the library for more than one afternoon a year. I never got in at all. We did all our work lying on our bunks, amid all the distractions and smells of dormitory life.

In spite of all these problems the teaching standards were good. We took copious notes and wrote essays that incorporated all that had been said. Most of the curriculum concerned Marxist philosophy, but we did have one course on western thought in which a foreign teacher taught us a bit about Christianity and liberalism. We learned it as well as we could, but of course did not take it seriously; it was simply more information to be presented in the next essay.

And so I drifted along for most of my first year at the university, not knowing that events were soon to blow my peaceful little world to pieces.

It all started with the death of Hu Yaobang on April 15. Some students began holding a vigil in Tiananmen Square, calling for a return to the kind of reforms for which Hu was known and respected. Most of these students were in their second or third year at the university and had demonstrated in early 1987 for more freedom—the very demonstrations that led to Hu's ouster on January 16 of that year. Somehow their vigil gained momentum. Word spread around campus that a big demonstration was planned and that the government would not object. The numbers grew, and the western press came running.

Soon the movement took on a momentum of its own. Students began to pour in from all parts of China and camped in the Square. We students from Beida kept voting to call off the demonstrations, but with so many of our counterparts from elsewhere still streaming in, we just couldn't bring ourselves to walk away and leave them to finish what we had started.

I joined the demonstration on May 5 without really knowing why. I knew next to nothing about democracy, and had little to say about how to improve society. I suppose there was a heady sense of excitement that we students just might influence policy for once in our history. We knew that China was in trouble. The graft and corruption were visible to everyone and were having a terrible effect on the country. If we could force the government to clean it up, then surely the future would be brighter.

When a million people thronged onto the Square on May 19 in support of the movement, we were thrilled. To listen to the reports of the BBC and hear of what we did . . . it was intoxicating. Even Gorbachev acknowledged us, and then Li Peng and Zhao Ziyang came to talk to us. We felt we could ask for anything. No one had any inkling of the carnage right around the corner.

It was on June 3 that something died within me. I suppose it was hope that died.

As it happened, I was nowhere near the Square. I was up at the Beida campus, a good hour's bicycle ride north of Tiananmen. It was late, about 11 P.M., and most of us were preparing for bed. Someone came tearing into the dorms shouting, "They're shooting us! They're shooting us!"

We knew who he meant, but we didn't believe him. It was preposterous. Surely the government would not respond with violence to unarmed civilians who were just making a point. But we had to find out. The whole month had been peppered with rumors, and we were determined to track this one down. Three of us leaped on our bicycles and pedaled furiously along the main street that led directly to Tiananmen Square. Sure enough, we could hear gunfire in the distance. As we continued to pedal at dangerous speeds down the dark, unlit street, thousands of others—ordinary citizens—were cycling alongside us, ignoring the government warnings over the radio to stay indoors.

I felt a curious exhilaration being a part of this cycling river. We felt like an army: quiet, determined, and rushing to battle.

But soon we found out we weren't an army. Far from it. An armored personnel carrier roared up the road ahead of us. Gunfire immediately erupted. We all dashed for the side streets, even fighting each other to get there first. My friend and I blundered onto another main street where students and young people were running in front of soldiers. We watched in horror from the shadows as soldiers calmly shot some of them at point-blank range, often in the back. Those they rounded up they handcuffed to trees or railings, giving them severe beatings, and leaving many bleeding and unconscious.

I was aware of a seething hatred for those soldiers. I wished fervently that I had a gun. I had never felt so enraged. My whole body seemed in the grip of an intense fear and hatred beyond anything I had experienced.

We picked our way back to Beida, avoiding the soldiers who had already surrounded the campus. I just lay on my bunk and wept. Wept from the shock of seeing my fellow students shot down like animals. Weeping, too, from futility. There was nothing I could do. Now we just had to wait for the government to round us up like sheep.

I wept all night, and three from our dorm did not return to their bunks.

I learned the next day that one of the three had been near the part of the Square where there had been a lot of shooting. I never saw him again. The other two were in jail. Nine months later, as I write this, they are still there.

Term broke up in chaos, and I prepared to go home to Harbin. A wave of bitterness swept through the students, a deep, smoldering resentment that etched itself on each face. I was frightened at this, as I had been of my murderous feelings the night of the massacre. I felt that these inner feelings were a force that could destroy me, and I didn't want to remain in their power.

That recognition provided the motivation to begin seeking some answers to questions that before had not bothered me. I could be bitter the rest of my life, or I could seek some meaning in areas that earlier I had ignored. The future that had seemed glorious when I passed my entrance exams now seemed impossibly bleak: more classes, more Marxist philosophy (which I now hated). Then the awful grind of trying to get an academic placement in the West. Exams again. That relentless treadmill! No thanks. I was in the mood to look for answers.

Back in Harbin I was able to get my father to pull strings again and managed to get into a library. I began my pilgrimage by sitting down at a desk and taking stock.

My starting point was that Marxism was useless. It justified the massacre with its teaching that the end justifies the means. I wanted to make sense of that evil, and to find an answer that could take away my anxiety and depression. In the quiet of the library, with no responsibilities or distractions, I could see that Marxism had been my religion. It was a creed, and I had had faith in it. Now I could either not have faith in anything, and maybe avoid a similar disillusionment, or I could transfer my faith to another creed. I wanted to do the latter because I was afraid of nihilism.

The point of getting into the library was that I could read old religious texts. I wanted to delve back into the history of Chinese religion and perhaps select one of them for myself. For the first few weeks I studied Taoism. But I found it to be completely egocentric and finally not much different from the nihilism that I feared. There was no remedy for bitterness within its teachings. Next I turned to Buddhism, which I found virtually indistinguishable from Taoism.

Then on to Confucianism. At first I thought I would get close to an answer. I was reading a passage from the biography of the Confucian statesman Chu Yuan (332-295 B.C.), where it said:

> Man came originally from God, just as the individual comes from his parents. When his span is at an end, he goes back to that from which he sprang. Thus it is that in the hour of bitter trial and exhaustion, there is no man but calls to God, just as in his hours of sickness and sorrow every one of us will turn to his parents.

This described my pilgrimage. The bitter trial of the June massacre was driving me to God. Somehow I felt I would succeed.

So what did Chu Yuan discover about God in his hour of trial? Imagine my disappointment when he said little about God, and my fear when I read that he committed suicide in despair. When I turned to Confucius himself, I still found no help. He was a wise man, but his wisdom was all of the common-sense kind. To follow his teaching might save one from foolish superstitions, but would do nothing to find God. Indeed, his followers seemed to take perverse delight in not knowing anything about God, but in nevertheless building a moral system in a void. This was no help. Its laws were easily broken, as the Chinese government had been doing with impunity, and there were no sanctions or other kind of help.

Then I picked up the *Odes*, a famous book of ballads on religious themes from ancient China. These were pre-

Confucian. To my surprise and joy, they did say something about God. They said he was One, and that he was spirit. But more surprising, I read that he was a God who could have a personal impact, and that he demanded standards of behavior that would bring judgment if they were not obeyed. For example: "It is not God that has caused this evil time, but it is you who have strayed from the old paths." This statement to the evil House of Shang thrilled me. Could there really be a personal God who held men accountable for their actions? But the *Odes* did not go further than that, and eventually you see the old emperors being deified and the notion of one supreme being getting pushed into the background.

That was as far as I got that summer. It was time to go back to Beida, this time a month earlier than usual for "ideological orientation."

The ideology classes proved to be predictably tedious. We dutifully obliged our instructors with "self-criticisms" of our roles last May and June. Actually we wrote little that would implicate ourselves, and were confident that even the teaching staffs were on our side.

More worrisome was the roundup of those involved in the pro-democracy movement. Many of my friends were in jail, and I knew that I was also on a government wanted list. But they knew how to play cat and mouse. As long as the government knew I knew I was on their list, they could be sure I would be on my best behavior and would not provoke them. The uncertainty only added to my fear.

Not long after returning to the university the pro-democracy movement reorganized, but it became more sinister. Weapons training and currency smuggling became part of it. To belong one must now be a desperado, ready to kill. Again this deterred me. I didn't want to take that route, to act like Lenin's definition of a revolutionary: a "dead man on furlough."

Still looking for answers, I reviewed the course I had already taken. I knew I had to look beyond China for a religion. But that religion had to do two things. First, it had to confirm that man is evil. I knew it because I had seen it, most convincingly in the massacres. Furthermore, I felt my own murderous instincts and wanted deliverance from them. This seemed to eliminate Hinduism from consideration. Like the Chinese religions, it seemed to affirm that man was basically all right, and it did not have a convincing basis for distinguishing between right and wrong.

Second, the religion I sought must tell me something about God himself. This was where I had found the Chinese religions so lacking. This also seemed to render Islam unsuitable, since it gives so little information about God.

Well, where else could I look but to Christianity? I felt like that poor fish in science class. I had tried to get to God through all other means, but each time it felt like a fin was being snipped off. All my careful study of Taoism, Buddhism, Confucianism, and classical Chinese religion had brought me hopelessly to the bottom of the tank, where I couldn't move.

But why was I so reluctant to consider Christianity? I don't know. Perhaps I was too proud as a Chinese and hesitated to find satisfaction outside my own culture. After all, if Christianity worked, would it be possible to be a Christian in a non-Christian country such as China? I had never met a Christian in China. I knew they existed, of course, and the following Sunday I headed off to a nearby Three-Self Church. To my surprise it was packed, with more than a thousand people crammed into the building. An even greater surprise was to see quite a number of student friends. I had assumed I was the only one with doubts, but obviously not. That made me feel a whole lot better about being in a church.

I remember little about the service. The singing seemed flat and the preacher extremely boring. However, what arrested me was the Scripture reading from John 8:23-24, "You are from below; I am from above. You are of this world; I am not of this world. I told you that you would die in your sins; if you do not believe that I am the one I claim to be, you will indeed die in your sins."

This verse came in the middle of an argument between Jesus and the Pharisees, who asked how he came to be speaking with such authority about God the Father. This was the very question I was also asking. Jesus clearly gave quite a lot of information about God, but why trust Jesus' definition? What made him any more special than Marx or Confucius?

The verse really hit my mind. What if Jesus did come from "above"? That would validate his information about God. It would mean that he was indeed more trustworthy than the various prophets.

I knew I had to get a Bible, and after the service I ordered one from the bookshop, although they said it would take some weeks to arrive. I went back to Beida with my mind ablaze with the staggering possibility that if Jesus Christ, who was a man, was also God, then my quest was over. Christ would have the answers all right. He had seen God in heaven. He was God himself!

During that week at class I was approached by an older student who said he had spotted me at church. After a brief chat he invited me to attend a meeting the following Sunday after the service, where a professor would talk about the Christian faith. "Say very little about it," he warned. "The professor holds these meetings quite unofficially, and the Three-Self authorities might not be too pleased to hear about it." For the first time I got an inkling that I was being drawn to a religion that could be dangerous. Clearly the Three-Self had to kow tow to the government. Might attending the class of this professor provoke the government into throwing me in jail?

For the next three days I sweated in an agony of indecision. But in the end I reasoned: *The government could arrest me anyway whether they have a valid reason or not. It's wrong to live in such fear of them. And anyhow, I need those answers.* So I decided, rather nervously, to attend the Three-Self Church again and go to the meeting afterwards with this professor.

The professor was a nuclear physicist, very well known, and reputedly with one of the brightest minds in China. Everyone knew that he had cut short a lucrative career in the United States to return home in 1955 in order to help with the rebuilding of China. The Communist Party thanked him by making him dig ditches for twenty years.

Now about seventy, he was restored to his academic post, and we students waited to hear what the great man had to say. We crowded into a small anteroom in the church. There were about twenty of us, and he held us spellbound with his brilliant apologetics for two hours.

He spoke mostly about the nature of truth, not relative truth which keeps changing, but the absolute truth that never changes. In order to be taken seriously it had to derive from a source who is still alive, unlike Confucius, Marx, or Mao. The only giver of truth still alive is Jesus Christ. He spoke of the connection between truth and love, with the only example of unconditional love extended to us in Christ, even though we do not deserve it. He spoke of the power of love that can change people. It is validated when it makes people better, and in this he claimed to speak from experience. "He has cleansed me. And I've never had to compromise. No philosophy or other religion can match that." Absolute truth also requires judgment. He was bold enough to talk about the Tiananmen Square killings as "massacres," and he said that God's judgment requires payment for all such events.

The professor then challenged us: "Is the truth you live by alive, loving, powerful, pure, just? Wouldn't you like to live by a truth like that? It's possible, but only Christianity has those characteristics. Try it for yourself."

I remembered that verse in the Gospel of John from the week before. Jesus Christ came from above. He is the embodiment of absolute truth.

As he spoke, his words seemed to burn painfully into my heart. He seemed to know all my fears. When he talked about Christian truth giving us the strength to love, my heart leaped. The truth that came from my own mind led to bitterness. It was without power and left me feeling futile. But the towering certainties of Christian faith that he explained overwhelmed me. Could there really be a truth that was never wrong, never inconsistent, never unjust, never unkind?

Perhaps what really convinced me was the professor himself. I had never heard a lecturer like him. He was animated. There was passion and conviction in his words. And halfway through his talk it suddenly occurred to me: "He believes every word he is saying." This was incomprehensible to me, being used to lecturers who hated what they had to teach. Not only that, but this man had personally tested these amazing claims of Christian truth, and was declaring them true in his own experience. I would have dismissed him if he were a peasant, but coming from one of the most intelligent men in China, it was impossible not to take him seriously.

I suppose that talk sealed my conversion. It was a voyage of discovery. I had reached Christian faith by encountering first all the dead ends of the other religions. I had made it home. Now I had a faith that could tell me what God was like.

As I learned to pray, I gradually felt the hatred leave my heart. I found love there instead. I could forgive Li Peng. I resisted joining the more subversive pro-democracy movement. I was now free without it.

I felt the fear leave me, too. I am no longer concerned about going to jail. I even attend a house church, which is forbidden in China. We meet secretly, sing quietly, and discuss the word of God in low tones.

There is talk of an imminent crackdown. But I have been delivered from fear. For months after the massacre I feared my own evil desires. I was a murderer in my heart, and was afraid that if the opportunity presented itself I would become a murderer in fact. And I was afraid of the government as well, of the pain it could inflict.

I am probably facing jail, or at least a lifetime of discrimination. But I pray my testimony will be like Paul's when he faced trial: "I eagerly expect and hope that I will in no way be ashamed, but will have sufficient courage so that now as always Christ will be exalted in my body, whether by life or by death. For to me, to live is Christ and to die is gain" (Philippians 1:20-21).

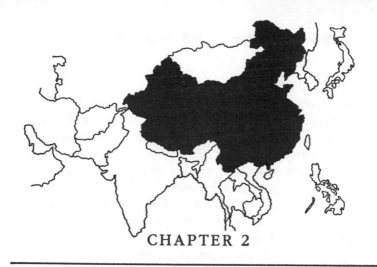

CHAPTER 2

ACTS, CHAPTER 29
by Kwan Ying

Introduction: Chinese civilization dates back to great antiquity. Its ancient glories included both monuments of high culture and brutal conquest. In modern times, however, decline and stagnation had become almost complete by the nineteenth century. In that period the general surge of Protestant mission work reached China and made important inroads. Catholics were also active.

Along with mission work the nineteenth century saw a renewed interest in China as a field of western colonialism. The low point perhaps was reached in 1900 when the Boxer (League of Righteous Fists) Rebellion failed to dislodge the Europeans who had established political and commercial enclaves on Chinese soil. Chinese rule was conducted more by local warlords than by formally constituted central government. The centralization process was undertaken by two opposing forces, the Communists and the Nationalists, beginning before the Japanese invasion of the early 1930s. This struggle ended four years after the defeat of Japan. In 1949 Communist forces took over China, forcing the Nationalist opposition to the island of Taiwan where it persists to the present under the name Republic of China.

As in the case of most Communist nations, China's constitution guarantees freedom of religion. And as in the case of them all, this paper guarantee fails to protect the right of Christians to worship and serve God as their faith requires. As the Communist party exercised its power over more and more of the country, it found an effective way to keep the church under its control. In the Three-Self Patriotic Movement (Protestant) and the National Patriotic Catholic Association (Catholic) it created tools through which it could ensure its domination over the churches. The authorities cut all ties with foreign churches and set up the Religious Affairs Bureau to exercise control over the Patriotic religious organizations. Since the RAB was subject to Communist party control, the party's grip on the Christian church was complete.

Or it would have been complete if the Christians had followed orders and confined their church activity to the official organizations. But numerous Christians believed it would be sinful to cooperate with such a scheme. Thus began the house church movement.

China suffered through a ten-year period of horrible brutalization called the Great Proletarian Cultural Revolution. This took place from 1966 to 1976, and stemmed from party leader Mao

Zedong's impatience with the bureaucratization and loss of revolutionary fervor into which the Communist party had fallen. He turned loose extra-official Red Guards who terrorized not only ordinary citizens but even high party officials. The most innocent gestures and statements might be interpreted as being bourgeois or capitalist or revisionist, and severe punishment meted out. Educational institutions were closed, economic enterprise suffered, and turmoil ruled. The suffering was enormous. This madness ended only after Mao's death.

The Cultural Revolution was especially hard on the church, with Christianity equated with foreign and anti-Communist ways. After it ended, information gradually seeped out that showed astonishing vitality in the repressed church. As recently as 1982, a highly regarded western reference work estimated the number of Christians in China at 1.9 million. This was an enormous understatement. Today the Three-Self Patriotic Movement admits to almost five million members, and many unofficial estimates put the true number as ranging up to fifty million. The many thousands of unofficial or house churches in China implicitly repudiate the state-approved church and show how the intentions of men are thwarted by the actions of God.

In the last few years the Chinese leadership has recognized that its policies have wrecked the nation's economy. The consequent liberalization of economic life has had important political and social repercussions. China has emerged from the depths economically, and more liberties are now permitted than in many years, although this process moves by fits and starts with many retrogressions.

Christians have benefited, as have all Chinese,

from the recovery, although by western standards there has been little of what might be called religious liberty. Government organs still control the churches, in some places much more than others. There is an ebb and flow to these matters and even before the 1989 bloodbath at Tiananmen Square many house churches felt renewed pressures from local officials. Often these officials are aided by Three-Self Patriotic Movement leaders who see the house churches as threats to their position.

Since the house churches threatened the efforts of the Communist regime to control all institutions, government policy centered on bringing all professing Christian groups under the jurisdiction of the official church bodies. The refusal of many of the church leaders, including Kwan Ying, to give in to the pressure and so compromise their loyalty to Christ set the stage for the brutal treatment which followed for almost three decades, and which still takes place.

• • •

I got down from a train in the Beijing railroad station and slowly walked down the platform. It was 1979. My heart pounded as I spied my family walking my way . . . and then right past me. They hadn't recognized me. And no wonder—it had been fifteen years since we had seen each other. Our reunion came after a long imprisonment and an even longer period of service to Christ that began a half-century before I got on the train.

I first moved to Beijing in 1928 when I was fourteen years of age. Western influence abounded in China at the time, and in my search for meaning in life I took classes at the YMCA. By then this organization had lost much of its Christian conviction and in its programs I heard only a gospel of social reform.

By the age of seventeen I was close to despair. Three things bothered me especially. The first was the meaninglessness of life. I found it hard to believe that all of life's significance could be found merely in the everyday world of school, work, and play. I was also unhappy about the lack of discipline of my classmates—they seemed spoiled (not that I was a better model). I wanted to overcome the sin that dominated my own life but saw no way to do it. Finally, I was obsessed about what happens after death.

In spite of the general failure of the YMCA to represent Christianity, two Christian teachers at the school greatly influenced me. Their inner peace showed on their faces, and they prayed much for me. I was a good student, and they seemed to take special interest in me. They often told me of the gospel of Jesus Christ. Finally, on December 29, 1932, while alone in my room, I turned out the light, knelt down, confessed my sin to God, and trusted in Jesus as my savior. Everything became new. I told all this to my schoolmates with great joy in my heart. I was eighteen years of age.

The next year I met some Christian charismatics. I went to two of their meetings but found them confusing. The third time, the Spirit filled me and I laughed for joy. I consider this to be the second blessing, although I did not speak in tongues. We have learned in China through many experiences not to be surprised at the workings of the Spirit, and we expect God to do miracles.

A year or so later I started attending Oriental Mission Society Bible School in Beijing and studied there from 1934 to 1938. American missionaries working with the Holiness churches ran the school. After I left I returned to the countryside where I worked with the Nazarene church as an evangelist. Communists there made it difficult to carry on.

At the end of four years I moved to Beijing with my family. After Japan surrendered in 1945 the American General George C. Marshall mediated between the

Chinese Communist party and the Kuomintang party under Chiang Kai-shek. These two parties set up a joint headquarters at the Beijing Union Medical College. They asked me to help them as a translator but I refused, thinking that it would distract me from serving the Lord.

When the property of the U.S. language school was given to a Danish missionary to be used as a hotel, I agreed to help for a short time as a cashier. For about three months I worked in the mornings and did church work in the afternoon. About that time a Norwegian missionary named Sovel came to the city for dental work. I taught him the Chinese system of music notation and that was the start of a collaboration between us.

At that time there were about sixty churches in Beijing. One of them was the Gospel Chapel. It had been started by a Japanese Christian after the occupation by Japanese armed forces. We bought a surplus U.S. Army jeep. Since it was used in the service of the Lord, we called it the first gospel car in the city.

One day Sovel and I drove to the city government office to get the Gospel Chapel registered. A Kuomintang official there thought Sovel was an American and therefore approved his request to register the chapel. Even though we didn't have any money, in a week we had opened the chapel. We paid the rent with grain.

Unfortunately, the relationship between Sovel and me soon ended. He wanted to put up a Pentecostal sign on the door, and I thought it would be too limiting. We couldn't resolve the disagreement, and as a result Sovel left—and with him the financial support for the ministry. Nevertheless, I began preaching the gospel in the street, supporting my family and ministry by translating for Americans who taught in the local Bible school.

Every summer we baptized some thirty to fifty converts from the street meetings. We also held Sunday services in the chapel and from 1947 to 1958 preached on radio programs. But after the defeat of the Kuomintang in 1949 and the Communist regime came to power, there were no more street meetings. In order to attract people into the building after that, I opened the front door and banged on a drum from just inside. This performed the same function for us as the bands used by the Salvation Army.

After 1949 all the missionaries were gone, and we were on our own. One YMCA leader in Shanghai—a patriotic Chinese but not a Christian—had a special interest in the place of the church in the new China. He also had friends in high places, including Zhou En-lai and the widow of the most famous Chinese in the early twentieth century, Sun Yat-sen. This man told us that the church in China had to cut all its ties with imperialism and establish itself as a purely Chinese church.

In 1950 the government put out a manifesto making it mandatory for churches to join the Three-Self Movement. Of the churches in Beijing, eleven refused to join, including mine. We saw no reason to make a show of severing ties with foreign Christians since we had already done so. We were on our own financially and in every other way. We also distrusted the leaders of the Three-Self Movement. We did not recognize them as spiritual leaders; many were Marxists or had adopted a theology opposed to the historic Christian faith. But the main problem with the Three Self Movement was its union of the spiritual power of the church with the temporal power of the state. These leaders made the church a tool of the state rather than a tool of the Holy Spirit, and we could not see how we could be part of it and still serve God.

The Communist regime labeled this refusal to join the Three-Self Patriotic Movement as anti-revolutionary. Beginning in 1955, pastors who did not join went to prison. The head of the Religious Affairs Bureau gave me some time to think it over when he locked up the other pastors because I was young and he thought I would change. But in the latter part of 1958 I went to prison, at forty-four years of age one of the youngest of the eleven. By then my wife was left with six children aged six to seventeen as well as my mother. They suffered greatly as the family of a counter revolutionary and were despised everywhere. My wife depended on the Lord to help her raise the children, and then she buried my mother.

In addition to the expected charge of refusing to join the Three-Self Movement and another one about refusing to join a political study group, the government said I was cheating my flock and making a lot of money. There was no lawyer, no defense, no jury. I received a life sentence. Another pastor also received life, with the others sentenced to fifteen to twenty years.

From 1958 to 1965 I was imprisoned in Beijing, assigned to work in a shop that made socks and plastic shoes. I could receive a visitor once a month for twenty minutes. When the prison became too full during my seventh year they moved me to a reform camp in the north of China—Heilungkiang Province, near the Soviet border.

The reform camp held about two thousand prisoners, all kept in one big building about 175 feet in length. A fire heated it at one end, but it was much colder elsewhere in the building. In the winter it got to about forty degrees Fahrenheit. We slept in a row, dormitory style. Prisoners of every type were there, from hardened criminals to political dissidents. But I knew of no other Christians in the camp, except for four Catholic priests. We did farm work for nine hours a day, with one day off every two weeks. At night we studied politics, reading newspapers for two hours and listening to politics on the radio.

Hunger stalked the camp. We were fed potatoes, barley, sorghum, and corn, sometimes a little cabbage. There was no meat or eggs. Prison guards beat and otherwise abused prisoners with the approval of our camp commander. Only enough medical treatment was given to keep prisoners alive; camp authorities were responsible for deaths.

I was accused of being both an American spy because of my "foreign religion" and a spy for Japan because the chapel had been started by Japanese. When these charges arrived in Beijing they made my wife's lot even harder. But she remained strong. She paid her tithe to the church all the time I was imprisoned, as poor as she was.

I had been mentally prepared before my arrest, so I didn't despair. I expected to spend the rest of my life as a prisoner. I never doubted God's love. I had many opportunities to tell prisoners about the gospel of Christ, but few were receptive. In twenty-one years only two prisoners came to Christ, as far as I know. I am still writing and sending literature to these two. Both are more than sixty years of age, single, and without a home. For the last seven years I have been sending them enough money to live on.

Deng Xiao Ping changed many policies when he came to power, including the one for prisoners. He released all the old soldiers of the Kuomintang who had been held since at least 1949. And he freed all prisoners over the age of sixty who had been in custody for more than twenty years. That is why I was taken from prison in 1979, after twenty-one years, and put on a train to Beijing.

After my release, I began serving a ten-year probation scheduled to end in October 1989. Amazing things have taken place in the years since I was imprisoned. The intense persecution has made the church very strong, and Christians all over the world are astonished at its growth. The Three-Self Movement claims there are about four million Protestant Christians in China, but the true number is many times that size. In spite of the government's continuing efforts to force all Christians into the Three-Self churches, most meet elsewhere.

Among Chinese Christians you find three attitudes toward the Three-Self Patriotic Movement Churches. The first is confrontation, in which people denounce the compromises of the church. A second group dislikes the

Three-Self Movement but takes part in it openly, using it as a cover to accomplish a genuine gospel ministry. The third group sees the Three-Self Movement as God's will. Those who hold this position seldom have an effective ministry. They have no power to affect the lives of people even if they are good preachers. A similar variation exists among pastors in the Three-Self churches. Some are good while others are self-interested and use the ministry to advance themselves.

Sometimes you hear the expression "underground church." But that is not the right term. We meet together in houses to worship the Lord. There is nothing underground about it. And there isn't much secret about it, although we do have to use discretion. No more than forty attend the church in my house, a very small residence with a single room. Young people make up more than half of our congregation.

Our fellowship meets on Sundays. We sing hymns and people speak as they feel led. There is no sermon, but there are testimonies, prayers, and Psalms. I also lead a Bible study and Sunday communion. We have to keep the noise down so as not to disturb the neighbors. Our house is in a row of similar houses, and we don't have enough space to meet our needs. We would like to find a bigger place to live and meet. When our numbers grow too large, we split off and start another fellowship. Although there is no organized effort between groups we know each other. We visit the sick and elderly.

I have found three ways in which to serve the Lord in my present circumstances. I receive visitors all the time, believers from many parts of China. I am able to give them books and Bibles from overseas. I help them understand how to serve the Lord and tell them to return to the book of Acts and follow in the footsteps of the apostles. At the same time I meet with people from other countries who come to my home. Or we meet in the city.

My second ministry is letter writing. I write about how to apply the Bible to modern life so people can serve the Lord faithfully. Once the mailman said to me, "There are 365 days in a year. You must get more than three hundred letters a year." One day I had six letters.

Third, I make cassette tapes. Many parts of China have no preachers. Believers gather around a tape player, listen to the message, and sing and pray. That is their worship service. Now we are starting to make video tapes. This is especially important for those who cannot read.

Because of my circumstances I have become well known among the Christians in China and even in foreign lands. People come here from all over our country for books and to learn how to serve the Lord. But we need many things in order to serve better. We need study Bibles, commentaries, concordances, biographies of great Christians, church histories, and so on. We need everything and have next to nothing.

Our biggest request of our brothers and sisters in other countries is that they pray for us. They should pray for the many millions of Chinese who are without Christ. They should pray for the multitudes of converts who are now being brought into the church, that we might have ways of edifying them even though we lack preachers and books. And there also must be prayer for the leaders of China, that they would give us a wide-open door for the ministry of the gospel.

We take much encouragement from the Scriptures. We know that the king's heart is in the hand of the Lord. We know that the gates of hell will not prevail against the church, as weak as it often seems. And while we know that the book of Acts has twenty-eight chapters, we believe that what is happening now in China is Chapter 29.

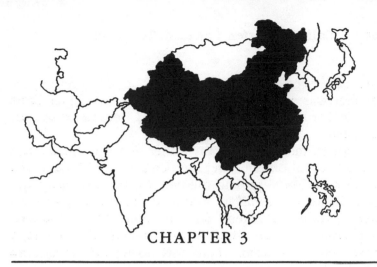

CHAPTER 3

LESSONS IN
LONGSUFFERING
by Li Wan

Introduction: After reading Kwan Ying's story in the preceding chapter, it is helpful to read one that contrasts so sharply with it. Li Wan's experiences are probably closer to those of the great mass of Chinese Christians. He has no dramatic story to tell of arrests, beatings, or imprisonment. But his family suffered greatly from persecution, and be himself has clearly been worn from the many years of job and educational discrimination, estrangement from companions in his community, and fear.

• • •

I am a third generation Christian who lives in the city of Xian. The believers in our family began with my mother's parents. My grandfather was converted through the efforts of foreign missionaries, and therefore my mother was reared in a Christian home. My father came to the Lord through my mother and became a zealous Christian.

Before the revolution my father was a professor and a government official. After the defeat of the Kuomintang he quit his job to go into full-time Christian ministry and began attending seminary. But in 1951, when I was three years old, he was taken from our home. I have only one impression of him when he was taken—a last hug. I never saw him again. There was no formal charge and no trial. He died in prison.

Later a fellow prisoner was released, came to visit my mother, and reported what had happened. The authorities warned my father not to preach Christianity to his fellow prisoners, but he persisted in obeying God rather than man. So they shot him.

This was very difficult for us to accept. I now believe that everything comes from the Sovereign Lord. He has prepared a unique life for each of his people and if life is hard for some of us, that is no reason to question the power and the love of God.

I was very young when I became a Christian. Once neighbor children beat me up in an alley without reason. When they began hitting me I dropped the stool I had been carrying. The back of the stool bore my name in my father's handwriting. I realized then that it was a Christian name—John. I was four years old.

After my father was taken I grew lonely and depressed. People regarded us as anti-revolutionary and despised the whole family. There were only two kinds of crimes—criminal and anti-revolutionary. It is still that way. For many of us our only crime is being a Christian, and for that we are regarded with suspicion and hatred. Ever since I have been sorrowful, and I believe it is because of the way our family has been treated. (On the other hand, my mother has a joyful disposition.)

I have always been under pressure for being a

Christian. Throughout childhood other children taunted me for being the son of a Christian. Their parents also would taunt me. Sometimes my mother would be harsh with me in order to help me get along better with neighbors. I now realize that the world hates Christians because we are not of the world. Those early experiences trained me in the New Testament virtue of being longsuffering.

After junior high school I could not get permission to enter high school despite my good grades. I started doing factory work and found that most of the heavy assignments were given to me. This discrimination came to me because of my father.

The contempt of my schoolmates was strongly influenced by a teacher who belonged to the Communist party. On breaks everyone rushed to the toilet. One day I slipped and hurt myself on the stairway, and without realizing it I bumped into another boy. He hit me. I did not return the blow although I could have done so. I realized that he was bold enough to hit me without reason because he knew that nobody would support me. This incident remained with me for a long time, along with the words of Jesus to turn the other cheek. It was very difficult to accept humiliation like this, but I remembered that Jesus also was mistreated. People do not know that Satan uses them to behave in this way.

Although I wanted to become a scientist I had no opportunity to do so. Instead I have worked hard as a laborer, and the Lord has used hardship to give me wisdom that I would not have otherwise gained. I have worked at the bottom of society for twenty years and have gotten to know that society well.

In China, big fish eat little fish. That is true in the factory in which I work. There are three men to a team in our factory, and we take turns resting. We only rest when we are told to rest, and often we work right through without breaks. It is easy to discriminate because everything depends on what the leader orders. Everyone wants to work less, but only those with a good relationship with the leader can do so. Since my file has followed me to this job I do not rest very often.

The Great Proletarian Cultural Revolution, which began in 1966 and lasted for ten years, terrorized many millions of Chinese. It was a fearful thing when Red Guards stormed the offices where citizens' files were kept. They found my file and discovered that I was a Christian and my father an anti-revolutionary. The file also reported that my grandfather and uncle were evangelists in Taiwan (which was not true). I had not made a public announcement that I was a Christian, but they found it out in the file. Every place I go the file goes with me, and that means hatred and ridicule follow. When I move I am well treated until the file catches up with me. It is like racism without race being a factor.

The church did not meet at all during the Cultural Revolution. Christians were separated from each other, and only a few close friends met together. We were able to help those who had family members in prison. The pressure on us was so great that only three things could be done in place of open worship: We visited each other, we had Bible readings within the family (although we had to hide the Bibles), and we prayed. We were thrown back on our individual relationship with God since there was almost nothing else to sustain us. Perhaps once or twice a year we would have meetings, but usually nobody but family attended.

After the fall of the Gang of Four in 1977 the Cultural Revolution ended and the educational system began to recover. The university held entrance examinations. Even though I had not attended high school I studied for the examination. Out of about sixty young people who took the examination, only ten passed. I was one of them. Eight out of the ten were admitted to the university. Of the other two, one woman became pregnant, and I did not pass the political examination.

In 1979 I enrolled in a different kind of higher

education—night school. Usually this does not lead to a degree, being a short-term course of six months to a year. In order to enroll I had to get permission from my work unit, which was refused many times. After two years the department that controls education approved my request, but my work unit still gave me a lot of trouble. They transferred me to a shift that made it almost impossible to attend classes. I had to change shifts with other workers. After much hardship I finally graduated with a degree in Chinese studies, which is rare in night school.

Getting a degree usually means getting a better job, but this has been impossible for me. China is very political. Since literature is used to promote political propaganda, the regime will not trust people like me to use it for the sanctioned purposes. Underneath the propaganda of the new order, China is still very feudal and patristic, very dependent on the traditions of the old society. It still associates the sons (and the daughters to a lesser extent) with the father's "misdeeds."

Nevertheless, my education was far from wasted. I love to read old western literature in translation—novels, criticism, Russian authors, biographies of Christians, Rousseau, Luther, Hudson Taylor, Bunyan's *Pilgrim's Progress*. I believe the Lord is using me right now, including my education. I often speak to people about God to counter atheist propaganda.

My brother is very good at working with his hands. He never did advanced study although he finished high school and passed his college exams. He was accepted by the university but it was a trap to get him out of Xian. He moved to the university town and then was refused university admittance. Since his residence was officially changed he could not return to our city. This was a bad year for Christians, and many preachers were arrested. During the Cultural Revolution my brother spent a year in prison, having been falsely accused of seeking revenge for our father's imprisonment and death. But he is a genius at fixing electronic devices; he is able to fix what no one else can. So he was called out of prison to return to his old job.

Party chairman Mao Zedong gave special instructions that skilled people like my brother should be rehabilitated. Premier Zhou En-lai said that people with a bad background who supported the Cultural Revolution were good, but the background was never forgotten. In this way the regime creates two classes of people. Because of this my brother never made it into management despite his great skills.

In 1981 some overseas Chinese Christians came to our city. One Christian sister visited us but was followed. I went out to the alley and saw two police in civilian clothes. When it was time for our friend to leave I took her to the bus stop by way of the alleys. We got on the bus at the last minute, and I got off at the next stop. The policeman who followed us went to my work unit the next day to question me and then talked to the manager. Nothing came of this, but there was not much they could do on the job since discrimination had already been in effect for a long time.

We are watched closely by neighbors, but we are willing to run the risk of meeting with other believers because we are edified and we have joy from meeting visitors.

Things are getting somewhat better now. The regime has been forced by circumstances into opening things up. When our pastor first came out of prison we did not meet. Now about seventy people meet in an apartment. We began meeting two years ago and meet every Sunday. There is singing, a sermon, prayers, and a benediction. We do not say anything against the government. There are people in the church who report to the government. When the Judases report, we usually find out about it. When we learn about such a person we just keep our distance.

Evangelism is all personal. Two years ago a relative

of one of the local Christians came to Xian and was converted. He went back and told people the gospel; now there are seven hundred Christians in his home town. Some foreigners who live and work in China are Christians and do effective work in evangelism. Many of our people are converted by listening to Christian radio from abroad. Also there are some good preachers in the Three-Self Patriotic Movement. Sometimes we go to the Three-Self Church on a Sunday if we hear that the preacher is good.

Still, we have no relationship with the Three Self Christians because their faith is different from ours. They act as if the authority of man is equal to the authority of God. They don't realize that the government, like everything else, is subject to God.

Radio broadcasts from foreign sources are very important to us. One relative from another city told us she had become a Christian by listening to foreign broadcasts. Some of the stations play all night long, and the hymns are a special comfort to us.

The suffering inflicted by the Cultural Revolution has made people more open to the gospel. Christian influence on the country is increasing as more and more people believe in Christ. When the work of the Lord increases there are fewer manifestations of the work of Satan. And when party members are converted it makes a great impact. The party tells them to choose between the party and the church. When they stand for Christ they lose their jobs. In the southwest part of the country, fourteen party members resigned together to be baptized—and the newspapers reported it. Events like this lead me to believe that Christianity is becoming a powerful force in China.

I believe that political pressures from the outside brought by Christians through their own governments can be a great help to us. But the main way our brothers and sisters in the outside world can help is by praying for us.

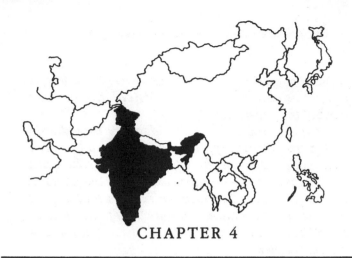

CHAPTER 4

LIFE OUT OF ASHES
by Vishal Mangalwadi

Introduction: The western world's image of India, based on perceptions of Gandhian pacifism as well as frequent press descriptions of India as the "world's largest democracy," is only partial and therefore very misleading. The Christian minority labors under forces that few western Christians understand. This is especially true for the rural areas where western newsmen do not normally penetrate.

It is deceptive to speak of India as a predominantly Hindu culture. Gandhi insisted that the untouchables be integrated with the general Hindu population, but this largely political gesture has not been implemented in the countryside. Untouchables are not welcome in Hindu temples, and their rights are breached more than honored. Partly as a consequence, the peasantry of India have seen the wealth drained from the countryside by political forces that control the government. [1]

Indian "socialism," the ideology that dominates the country, allows those who can manipulate the system—politicians, bureaucrats, and businessmen—to gain wealth at the expense of everyone else. Christian ministries that expose the system at the same time they help people can expect the kind of opposition that we read about in this chapter.

• • •

*I*n 1976 my wife Ruth and I went to live in the village of Gatheora in the central part of India, a town of about two thousand residents. There is a big difference between the city and the village in India. Our village has no police station, no press, no civil servants, no telephone. Many villages don't even have electricity. And there is no political structure in the usually accepted sense, although there are plenty of opportunities to play politics.

Thirty years earlier, about the time I was born, my father bought a plot of land in that area. He was a Christian pastor and had prayed for the area for many years. Ruth and I caught his vision; you might even say we inherited it. We wanted to make it an outpost for Christ, a kind of beachhead in the midst of dark paganism.

At the time we lived in the city of Alhabad, where my father served as secretary of the Bible society. Even though it was his vision we desired to put into action, he opposed our moving to the village. We moved there anyway.

One of our first contacts there turned out to be quite important. A man by the name of Khubchand had made a profession of faith in Christ under my father's ministry many years before. But under constant pressure from his Hindu friends and neighbors he had recanted and had been living as a Hindu. Christians in the area had written him off and had no contact with him. But my father had not forgotten him, and every time he went to the village he visited Khubchand. When Khubchand heard that Victor Mangalwadi's son had moved to the area he decided not to visit us, assuming that we would shun him just as the others had done.

A second important contact also enters the story here, an old man who had been one of the first in the area to become a Christian. He had suffered serious persecution, and his wife had left him because of his faith in Christ, but he remained unshaken. He used to sit on the pavement in the town and sell clothing, keeping his Bible handy. If those who bought clothes from him were from his caste, he would talk to them about the Lord.

The old man died, and Khubchand attended his funeral. It was a hot day in June, and Ruth asked him to come to our house for a glass of cold water. He came and sat with us, and Ruth made him a mango drink. This thrilled him, so different was it from his life as an untouchable since his return to Hinduism sixteen years earlier. We did not realize until later how important this was to him. It made him open once more to consider the gospel.

"Your friend remained faithful and then died," I said to him, "and there is a crown for him in heaven. But you've turned back. You're old, you are going to die soon, and because you've turned away from the Lord you know where you are going." That direct witness, plus Ruth's hospitality and being treated with respect, made him think seriously about his life.

Four days later he returned. "After I went from here the Lord convicted me," he said. "I have sinned. I have spent the last three days in the fields in fasting and prayer. I have just gone to the district magistrate and resigned. Now I'm going to work with you." He had been a gardener in the district magistrate's residence, but now he thought his spiritual decision meant he must quit that job and work with us. At the time we were ourselves in difficult straits economically. But we did not give in to the temptation to brush him off, believing that the Lord could take care of us in whatever way he wished. So we answered: "All right, we have no money, and we can't offer you any salary. But if we eat, you will also eat."

With that agreement made, he said, "We'll begin evangelism tomorrow. I will come at six o'clock in the morning and I will take you to see a friend of mine." We didn't take him literally, especially since he had to come eight kilometers on his bicycle. But the next morning, even though it was raining, he showed up at the time he said he would. We visited the first man, and Khubchand told him his story. That man trusted in the Lord, and our evangelistic work had begun. A few weeks later he went on his own into our village and talked to men of his own caste—untouchables—and they too came to Christ. Then he brought them to me, and I taught them from the Scriptures. They said they wanted to be baptized so we organized the first baptism ceremony. Other conversions followed.

All were poor men to whom credit was an important part of their lives. But now that they had become Christians their credit dried up; no one would lend to them. Under pressures like these some of the converts recanted and went back to Hinduism. In one case a man's wife was about to give birth, and nobody would help him. No doctor lived in the village so he reconverted to Hinduism in order to get care for his wife.

Shortly after that my father and I took a walk in the village. We came upon a slightly higher caste Hindu sitting in a tree cutting a branch. I introduced my father to him and said, "This is Durjan," which means literally "a bad man." My father looked at him and said, "You're Durjan, you must become Sajjan." (You're a bad man, you must become a good man.) He was half-joking, but the words pierced that man because he *was* a bad man. He had been a robber for two years, although my father hadn't known it. Durjan was familiar with the gospel because he knew Khubchand's friends and was following the evangelistic effort. He took my father's half-serious remark in the light of everything else, and a few days later he came to me and said: "I am a bad man. How can I become a good man?" He became a Christian.

This conversion angered people in the village. Some high-caste men burned down the fence around Durjan's fields. Then they burned down his house. These houses have mud walls and a wooden frame for the roof, with twig and clay tiles piled on, so there is a lot to burn. When the roof burns, the whole structure collapses and destroys the family's food, which is devastating. This man and his wife suffered much (she also became a Christian) but they didn't renounce their faith. Still, the suffering of Durjan was so great that it dissuaded others from considering Christianity. The church has not grown much in that village.

Some time later, in 1980, we began to evangelize tribal peoples in our area. Two men joined us as part-time evangelists, and soon thirteen tribals from one village were converted. But when they returned home the villagers destroyed their Bibles, beat up their leader, and threatened to kill them. Although the intimidation was severe we hoped to support them by sending two brothers to help. When one of the two had to return to his family for a time, a Moslem volunteer replaced him temporarily in order to distribute seed. This man had become very interested in our work, especially when we began a relief program (a serious drought plagued the area).

These two people, the Christian and the Moslem, lived in Nagod, a town near the tribal village. As they slept one night a knock came at the door. It was about 3 A.M. The Moslem opened the door and was immediately attacked, having been mistaken for one of the evangelists. The visitors pounced on him without saying a word, swinging axes, and when they were finished left him for dead. He survived much bleeding and many stitches in his head with the loss of an ear and with continuing pain. No legal action was taken because nobody was willing to testify against the attackers.

The attack accomplished its intended purpose. Nobody else went to that village to encourage the new converts, and the outpost gradually faded away. Only in the last few years have we been able to send workers back in, and once again new converts are coming to the faith and a worshiping group has been established. We have learned that persecution can be very effective, especially with new Christians.

Meanwhile, back in our own area, more and more people showed interest in the gospel and were coming to Christ. A number of these new Christians began making an economic contribution to the community and gradually began to be lifted out of the poverty into which the area was sunk. While this gratified us and served as another validation of the gospel, it brought with it a serious problem. Some people misunderstood our message and assumed we wanted them to follow us personally, and if they did so we would give them jobs and see that they were taken care of economically. They didn't believe us when we told them we had no material riches to offer. When they realized the truth of the matter they immediately reverted to Hinduism. They became some of our severest critics.

By then, some 100 to 150 people were coming to worship services. But very few Christians lived in the villages; most were concentrated in the cities. All of them were untouchables and therefore were not allowed in the Hindu temples. (That they were officially considered Hindus is a political fact, not a religious one.)

About seventy of these men came from the biggest village in the area where there remained a strong remnant of the old feudal system. The descendants of the local kings and their *jagirdars*, or tax collectors, form the power structure of the village. These *jagirdars* are sometimes called "little kings." The little king of that village had large political ambitions. He was an immoral man, making his money by illegal means, and he found his situation humiliating—it reflected badly on him that seventy men from his village attended Christian worship services. By this time we had baptized about eighty people, some of them phony Christians, some of them real ones who would collapse under Hindu pressure, and some genuine believers who would stand fast despite everything.

In 1979 devastating storms hit our normally dry area. Many dams burst in the floods that followed. Ruth and I were sitting in our room when the water started spurting through the mud joints between the bricks. It looked like a shower. The whole region suffered great hardship. We were convinced that our responsibility was to bring as much relief as possible.

We concentrated on villages which suffered from collapsing houses. Following the advice of several international Christian relief agencies, we worked through the existing power structure. We asked village chiefs to choose the families most needy of help, and the relief money was handed to those families by the chiefs in our presence. The chiefs got the credit, of course, but we were satisfied there had been no corruption. We learned later that the chiefs had been paid off in advance; the relief money in effect had gone to the highest bidders.

The next year a severe drought hit. We got into a food for work program funded by an ecumenical group. We furnished powdered milk to children and nursing mothers. We also put a thousand people to work repairing roads and deepening wells and ponds. We learned from our previous mistake and chose people to work with us who were willing to develop a special relationship with us. Most were of the priestly caste, which technically was higher than the chiefs, but these people had no political position. The program was highly successful. The people noticed that they were paid on time, in the full amount, and did not have to pay off anyone in charge. That was a sensation.

But in India everything is political. The chiefs got together with the "little kings" and decided to oppose us. Our men were becoming well placed politically, and that threatened these men's political and economic base. They set to work on the district magistrate and before long the government withdrew permission for our work. We made numerous appeals, but the magistrate always spouted some pretext for refusing us permission. The funding agency required permission from local authorities for relief efforts, and they began putting pressure on me. If I could not get the signature I needed, they would have to withdraw all financial and material support. Finally that is what happened, and the relief work ceased. Then the authorities started six court cases against me for "illegal possession of public dams and wells" which we were repairing. Some of these cases are still pending eight years later.

About a month later the drought ended and economic life began returning to normal. We became embroiled in a struggle in which a Christian was trying to recover land that was legally his but which a wealthy high-caste man was occupying. A common situation in India: a man has an impeccable case before the law, but people with wealth and power override the law. Many thousands of wealthy people get their property from its rightful owners while the legal system and the police stand by and do nothing.

But this time the religious angle also entered. About a hundred of these men who had unjustly obtained property got together to take action. They reasoned like this: "If this one man can get his land back with the help of Christians, it will go hard for the rest of us. The

Christians will gain many converts and many will be out to get their land back in the same way. It could open the floodgates." They vowed solemnly not to allow any Christians to take root in their area. Thus the religious issue got dragged into the question of justice. It shows how economics, politics, and the spiritual battle all become mixed together.

My father had settled in the village by then, and these men said to him: "Tell your son to keep out of this, or the consequences will be very bad." My father, being a pastor, gave them moral lectures. But they kept threatening. I was living about eight kilometers away from that village in the community we were building up.

Ruth and I had been invited to go to Holland to give a series of lectures. The night before we left, about 9 P.M., a man knocked at my father's door, claimed to be from the electricity department, and asked to check the meter. He looked the place over, let in two others, and all three beat up my father. They ransacked the place, then tied my father to a chair, beat up my stepmother, and raped the young girl living with them. Then they took out a knife and threatened to gouge out my father's eyes (a common practice in our area). They said they would allow him to keep his eyes if he would give them all the money he had in the bank. He agreed. They also made him promise to move away from the village work altogether.

At the time I knew nothing of this. The next morning as we packed my father came to say goodbye. He was very serious but we couldn't tell why. After he sent us off he went to the bank, withdrew all his money, and handed it over to the criminals. Then he filed an informal report with the police department, which took no action. Three weeks later we learned what happened when my father wrote to explain it all.

The experience shattered my father. He had looked forward to living on his own farm and establishing churches in the area. Now his dream lay in ruins and his money had evaporated.

Also about that time my aunt and uncle were murdered—stabbed to death in their own home. To this day I do not know the extent to which all these incidents may have been connected. But the cumulative effect was to demoralize the band of believers who were trying to evangelize the district. Evangelism screeched to a halt. Everyone wanted to run away. My father and others tried to prevent Ruth and me from remaining in the area, but we doubted the theory of a conspiracy. We felt that if there was a conspiracy, it was in the heavenly realm, and we had the means to withstand it through the Lord's help.

I did not put any pressure on Ruth about going back to the village, but she prayed about it and one morning decided that she did not want to allow her fears to dominate the decision. Right afterward she received a phone call from an Australian woman affirming her desire to come to the area as my secretary, but only if Ruth were there. We took that as a tremendous confirmation of Ruth's decision. Our friend and colleague Shourie also determined to stay with us. If that meant bullets, he said he was ready to take the first one.

It seems paradoxical that in the midst of great problems with fearful Christians we also saw a movement of the Spirit. One of our original converts, after having been expelled from our community for stealing, had repented of his sin and returned to the Lord. While we were gone he had actively witnessed to his friends about the grace of God, had dealt with cases of demonic possession, and without being in contact with fellow Christians had been doing the work of the ministry. When we returned from Delhi to the village, coincidentally he got on the bus we were riding and told us of his experiences. He begged me to return with him and begin teaching the new converts.

When I returned I asked my father to baptize them, but my parents' dreadful experience had just taken place. He had to fight off my stepmother's insistence that he not take part in such a provocative action. Nevertheless, he acceded to my wishes and baptized the new converts. This took place in January when the waters were very cold. Soon after my father became ill and eventually died. My father's death hit us hard, coming on top of all our other troubles. No one could replace him in evangelistic work. At about the same time another effective evangelist also died. I was spending a good deal of time in economic projects—in farming, poultry raising, and blanket and carpet weaving—so that the Christians could enjoy and demonstrate the economic fruit of a life devoted to Christ.

We made many mistakes in those days, partly because we labored under the handicap of false ideas. Socialist thinking is so ingrained in the Indian consciousness that almost without thinking people assume that profit-making enterprises are immoral. Consequently, our projects were communal in nature, and that meant no incentives to work hard and intelligently. I constantly had to solve management problems that would have solved themselves had socialist ideology not permeated our organization. That meant I could not devote sufficient time and energy to helping the faltering churches.

In spite of these difficulties we tried to press ahead and achieved some successes. In March 1982 our area suffered a devastating hail storm which destroyed the crops around thirty villages. That night I was in the hospital and heard patients from surrounding villages cry for their crops and houses. I prayed that the Lord might help us provide relief. The next morning a visitor from a Christian relief and development organization came to see me. We regarded that as an answer to prayer.

Soon he had the area surveyed and the project planned and had secured funding from his organization. About four or five days had gone by and the government had done nothing, not even offered its usual empty promises. We began to advertise in the newspapers, advising people to apply to us for aid. The press gave us big coverage and used it as a stick to beat the politicians. The "little king" who was then a member of the legislative assembly suffered deep humiliation. The politicians were seen as insensitive to human suffering while we were considered compassionate and effective.

The local legislator therefore moved to head off further political damage. He got the district magistrate to ban the relief effort. We replied that we would hold a prayer meeting for all the villagers, asking God to comfort the afflicted. But they understood we would also inform the people why there would be no material help from us. They feared that thousands of people would gather to pray and that the government would relent and allow us to distribute relief. So they banned the prayer meetings on the grounds that they would disturb the peace.

By this time our opponents sent the district superintendent of police to persuade me to accept their point of view. He spent three or four hours threatening me, promising that if I continued to make trouble they would eliminate me. I went home to pray and concluded that God was testing our commitment to the poor. So I went to the district officials and told them we would have to continue with our plans for the prayer meeting. We invited the politicians and officials to attend.

Twenty-four hours before the prayer meeting the police arrested me. The next day they arrested twenty-six of our people. This marked the beginning of a new phase of opposition. After I had been in jail for five or six days the press began to bombard the government and they had to let me out. They offered to release me on bail but I refused. They released me anyway because the press was generating too much heat. We decided to have prayer meetings in all the villages and to go on with relief work in spite of the government's ruling. If they wanted to stop us with force they could do so.

For a week I walked through the whole area from village to village, a distance of about three hundred miles. Whole villages came out, and we sang songs, talked to them about the gospel, and told them what happened to the relief work. The people responded overwhelmingly. The day we started distributing relief supplies I was arrested again.

The police charged me with holding a revolver on a man and threatening to kill him unless he became a Christian. Later I was arrested again on a charge of rape. The first case is still pending, although the man never came to court to present evidence. The woman who lodged the rape complaint is the man's wife. That case was dismissed due to lack of evidence; the police record did not even show a medical examination.

At about the same time I was harassed in another way. It is common in India for politicians to use the court system for political purposes. Local politicians induced the district magistrate to charge me with several crimes, all fabricated. They hoped to force me into wasting my energy and money in fighting these contrived charges and thereby prevent me from carrying on the ministry.

We ascertained that this harassment came from a group of five village chiefs working with a member of the legislative assembly whose constituents worshiped with us. It was this politician's caste that had grabbed the untouchable's land; they were afraid that their rule of oppression was endangered.

The truth is that their domination *was* endangered. We did not go into ministry with political goals, and I did not even belong to a political party, but they could see the explosiveness of the gospel. Untouchables make up the vast majority of the population and yet are exploited and robbed at will, largely because they see no alternatives. But the gospel teaches them that they are equal, not untouchable. We befriend them and invite them to eat with us. This undercuts the legitimacy of the social order. So the high caste and politicians are right to see us as a threat, even though we do not preach or organize against them.

Tension grew thick. Their threats to kill us were tempered by increasing public and press support for us. That's when they developed another tactic. They wrote to the foreign organization funding our relief work and told them that we were using their funds for political purposes. The organization sent auditors who went through our books and found the charge baseless. But the organization's leadership grew worried that they might be blacklisted in India, so they backed out of their agreement with us.

When it began to appear that I was acting as a lightning rod for the opposition, I resigned from the organization's Indian branch. The organization said our presence in the area would hinder the new leadership, so they asked Ruth and me to move out of the area. We moved our family to Mhow, in the western part of the state of Madhya Pradesh.

And then a great irony developed. The legal cases that had been filed against me in order to stop the work of the ministry forced me to return to the area repeatedly in order to defend myself. Every time I came I was able to help with the evangelistic work. At the same time I built an organization called Society for Service to Peasants. After about eighteen months the original ministry was ready to collapse, and I was asked to return to a leadership role. Not long afterwards a Christian research organization in Delhi asked us to take over its operation. Since the owners of the house in Mhow were returning we had to leave anyway, so we moved to Delhi in April 1984.

The next November our whole community at the village was burned down.

It is easier to understand what happened if you recall the political situation at the time. In October 1984 Mrs. Gandhi was assassinated. Her Sikh guards killed her, triggering massive riots and violence against Sikhs.

Thousands were killed. Much of the violence was directed by Congress Party politicians. In our area the reasoning seemed to be: "While we're permitted to kill the Sikhs, we might as well get rid of the Christians." So about eighty men raided our community and systematically set fire to the houses, tractor, ambulance, and motorcycle. About thirty people lived in the community at the time. The raiders beat up some of our men, and the society lost about 900,000 rupees worth of property. I lost the personal library I had collected over the years.

Since then, some of the buildings have been reconstructed but only about ten or fifteen people live there. The greater blow to us was psychological; out of fear few people associate with us. Of about one hundred people who had been baptized, only forty or fifty are now willing to be known as Christians.

It is now more than three years later, and Christian activity is beginning to pick up again. Two evangelists are active in the area. Our people have begun a school, and the followers of Christ are coming to life out of the ashes of the old community. We are much encouraged that the Lord is rebuilding the work. And while there has been no active persecution recently, we know that may change since the Christian community again has come to life and is expanding.

Notes

1. Even the most sympathetic analyses of the Indian economic situation dwell at length on the damage that corruption does both to the poor and to the whole economic system. See, for example, the work of the Nobel prize winning Swedish economist Gunnar Myrdal, *Asian Drama: An Inquiry into the Poverty of Nations*, 3 vols. (New York: Pantheon, 1968). Those interested in a Christian approach to the issue of economic development of poor countries may consult Marvin Olasky, Herbert Schlossberg, Pierre Berthoud, and Clark H. Pinnock, *Freedom, Justice and Hope: Toward a Strategy for the Poor and the Oppressed* (Westchester, Ill.: Crossway Books, 1988).

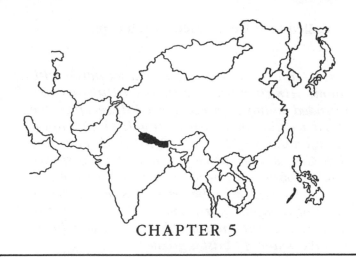

CHAPTER 5

SPIRITUAL WARFARE
IN KATHMANDU
by Tirtha Thapa

*Introduction: The context in which Nepalese
life takes place is strange to a westerner in many
ways. But perhaps nothing is stranger to someone
living in a secularized society than the
pervasiveness of the* spiritual *in a country like
Nepal. This is a spirit-drenched community, a
sense that fills the consciousness of almost the
entire population. People are not aware of any
vacuum for the gospel to fill. Rather, the gospel hits
them as an alien force that crashes against a
hardened block of religious conviction. This
accounts for some of the hostility that new
believers face, not only from the government, but
also from friends and family.*

*Moreover, the Nepalese are intimately
connected to the spirit world. They believe that
many of their sicknesses are caused by demonic*

*forces, and most Nepali Christians agree with
them. Hindu rituals and incantations are
intended mainly to protect the worshipers from the
spirit world. Christian evangelists call upon
manifestations of the Holy Spirit to demonstrate
that God is more powerful than the evil spirits.
This emphasis is found in many countries, of
course, but seldom to the extent it is true in Nepal.
Fear of demons is a formidable deterrent to
accepting Christ until people become convinced
that the power of Christ is greater.*

*Nepal's mountainous terrain and sparsely
settled countryside make the problem of
conversion more difficult. Traveling to the next
village can mean days of walking over rugged
terrain, and the isolation cements each village
into a tightly closed community hostile to what it
regards as deviant thinking. For someone to
profess Christ in the village is not only a serious
matter for the religious tradition, it is also taken as
a repudiation of the convert's family and
neighbors. It is a rejection of his whole
community. And since it can be a week's walk to
the next Christian, the hardship and suffering of
professing Christ is made especially acute by
isolation.*

*Tirtha Thapa has become one of the
acknowledged Christian leaders in Kathmandu
and is president of the Nepal Christian Fellowship.*

• • •

I was born in a village in the western part of Nepal. I
have been interested in religion since I was a small
boy. Because our village was Hindu, it was natural that
my interest should lie in that direction. But by the time I
arrived at college in Kathmandu I had become an atheist.
In a society like ours, in which religion penetrates

everywhere and so much depends on it, it sometimes seems better not to show your atheism openly. So I was an atheist on the inside but a Hindu on the outside.

At the university I met someone who told me about the gospel of Jesus Christ, but I had a hard time believing him. When the only religion you have known is Hinduism, the strangeness of the Christian message is not quickly overcome. A tremendous gap lies between a religion ruled by fear of spirits and one that relies wholly on God's grace to make possible inner peace. This friend gave me a New Testament, and I began reading it.

In God's providence one passage of the New Testament impacted me twice in the same day. I read in Romans 3 that all men are sinners and that they fall short of God's standards. By that time I had begun attending a Christian church, and the very day I read that passage the pastor preached on it. The idea angered me because I did not believe I was a sinner. It seemed to me that my long-standing interest in religion, and the fact that I participated in Hindu ceremonials, made me different.

But that night, in bed, I prayed that if God were real he would show me that I am a sinner as the New Testament said. For the rest of the night I recalled numerous incidents from my life, many long forgotten. That is how I realized that the biblical teaching of man as sinner applied to me as much as to anyone. It was then that I trusted in Jesus and asked him to forgive my sins. That night I became a Christian. It was nine years ago.

Two years later I returned to my village in the countryside. Our village lies in the western part of the country and is somewhat isolated, although not nearly as much as others—many of which can be reached only by walking over the mountains for a week. You could drive to ours if you had a four-wheel-drive vehicle (which none of us do). About fifteen hundred people live in our village.

I told my family and my neighbors about Jesus, and they stared at me in disbelief. My family would not allow me to enter the house. They said I was a very low person, an outcast. Some neighbors began hitting me. After two days I was driven from the village.

Slowly, I rebuilt a relationship with my family so at least I could talk to them. Eventually they changed their mind about my faith because they saw the power of Christ in me.

The villages suffer much from demon possession. Villagers fear evil spirits and for this reason witch doctors have great power over them. Once I visited a member of the family who was ill. The witch doctor came but refused to do anything until he was paid. The family asked me to pray that the sickness would leave. My family turned to Christ when they saw that the prayer of a Christian would heal the sick person; the demon was cast out and did not return. So my family wanted to know more about what had happened to me. I gave them a Bible and soon after their attitudes changed. Four years after my own conversion all of them believed in Christ.

When my family came to faith, the whole community turned against them. They even kept us from taking water from the common stream because they thought we would contaminate it. Anyone who came into our house was cut off from the community, so we became isolated. It was especially hard during religious festivals, because that is a time of special community feeling. When people walk into the village they read on the stones that these people have become Christians, that they eat cow, that they worship the pig. In this case my family came to no physical harm. In other places Christians have been beaten, their houses torn down, their crops set on fire, or their livestock killed. But still the mental torture has been great. More than anything the isolation brings great suffering.

They are the only Christian family in the village. The nearest church is about one day's walk away. I am buying some land in Kathmandu and will bring them here so they don't have to live any longer in that terrible isolation.

Persecution of Nepali Christians generally takes place on three levels. The first level is in the family. Hinduism has millions of gods, but individual families have particular ones they worship. The idols are found in the kitchen, and everything the family eats is offered first to the idol. So for a new Christian just to eat with his family presents a serious moral problem. It is also a problem for the family; when a Christian enters the kitchen the family considers it defiled.

The second form of persecution takes place in the community. Neighbors think you have not only changed religions, but that you have deserted the community and shown contempt for everyone in it. This explains my family's difficulties.

The third level of persecution is the legal side. We want the government to stop jailing and beating us, but that will not by itself change what happens in the family and the community. Still, when the law of the land stops discriminating against Christians, we think it will have an effect on the way ordinary people treat us.

It is important to know these things in order to understand what happens to Christian families in the villages. Unlike many other parts of the world, there is no regular legal system to provide some measure of security. ·

For the most part the Nepalese government has not encouraged persecution in the villages, but neither has it discouraged it. The remoteness of the villages allows life to go on with little influence from the outside. The local authority is a headman, who is elected by the village council of elders. His role is something like the king of the village. There is no police force and no representative of the Nepalese government. It is a two-day walk to the nearest police authority, so if there is a crime (such as the theft of a pig) the headman usually takes care of it. He may order the thief to be beaten or to make restitution. Even after these punishments the headman can still turn the criminal over to the courts for more punishment.

A couple of years ago at our first Christian law conference we were trying to educate believers about their rights under the law. Most of our people do not understand it. One pastor was arrested a short time after the conference and said, "I'm a Nepali and I have rights under the law. I want to see your warrant for my arrest." The policeman, who had not taken our course, replied: "Oh, you want to see my warrant, do you?" Then he took out his stick and hit the pastor on the head. "That's my warrant. Let's go." By asking that his rights guaranteed under Nepali law be respected, he got the police stick instead.

So it is for now. But by God's grace and through the prayers of his people, we have hope that our situation may soon improve.

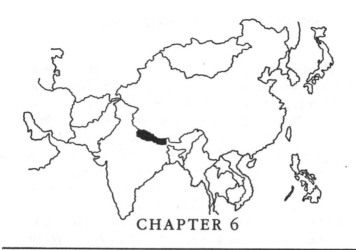

CHAPTER 6

WHEN CHRISTIANITY
AND HINDUISM COLLIDE
by Charles Mendies

*Introduction: Nepal is a long, narrow land
dominated by a spiny ridge of high mountains
and situated between Tibet and India. This
ancient nation is little known in the west except
for its mountains and trekking expeditions. One
reason for its obscurity is that until 1951 Nepal
was officially closed to foreigners. Since the
country opened itself up, there have been many
evidences of outside influence. In the capital city
of Kathmandu, for example, many stores advertise
their names and wares in English as well as in the
native script.*

*The kingdom has few western notions of
legality. As Charles Mendies points out, jury trials
and the prohibition against double jeopardy are
absent in Nepal. And unlike most modern nations
which persecute Christians, Nepal makes no*

pretense of religious liberty. It is constitutionally a Hindu kingdom, and the official persecution which takes place is a function of its laws.

Religious typologies sometimes suggest that Hinduism is one of the "higher" religions, but that is serious error. The Hindu pantheon includes innumerable gods and goddesses. In practice it is a religion of terror and idol worship. Fearful devotees try to propitiate demons in order to protect themselves from natural disaster and disease. By driving just a short distance from Kathmandu the modern visitor can see the animal sacrifices that testify to this. Long lines of people wait their turn to appear before the priests and their assistants. Most are leading goats, chickens, or other small animals. Some of the poorer people can only afford flowers as their sacrifice. After prescribed incantations the priest's assistant kills the animal with a knife and holds it up to the idol so the still-beating heart can pump the blood over the image. The animals are then taken to another part of the sacrifice grounds where they are butchered.

It is only when you get beneath the bare visual image of the scene that the true horror becomes clear. The people are convinced that evil spirits are ready to bring misfortune on them, and sacrifices are the only way they know to mollify the demons. Terror dominates them. When these people come to faith in Christ they are freed from bondage in a way that few westerners can fully appreciate.

Christian missionaries first arrived in Nepal in 1952. A number of Indian Christians have entered Nepal to conduct ministries there. Missionaries are not officially welcome in the country, except for the United Mission to Nepal which is staffed by a number of foreign mission agencies. Their work is officially confined to

*medical, engineering, and education tasks, with
no preaching permitted. It is impossible to find out
exactly how many Nepalese are Christians, but the
figure forty thousand out of a population of about
fourteen million is sometimes mentioned. At best,
that is a guess.*

*Charles Mendies, although a young man, is
one of the best-known of the Christian leaders of
Nepal. He and his colleagues have been in the
forefront of Christian evangelism in the country.
He has been particularly active in literature
ministry in the villages. As this is written, he has
been out of prison for only a few days, freed by the
bloody revolution that forced the king to begin the
democratization process. There are rumors that
the new constitution will include provisions for
religious liberty, but nobody can say right now
what will happen.*

• • •

Although I was born in Kathmandu, the capital of
Nepal, and have lived here almost all my life, I don't
look like the typical Nepali. The reason is that my father
is an Anglo-Indian and my mother comes from Canada.
She traveled to India as a young woman to serve as a
Salvation Army missionary, and she and my father met in
the mission. Shortly after they married, Nepal opened up
to foreigners. Until 1951 the Kingdom was closed to
almost all outside influences. The few cars in the country,
all in Kathmandu, were carried over the mountains on
the backs of laborers. All the fuel and spare parts came in
the same way.

When the country was opened my father was invited
into Nepal to start a hotel, his business in India. He
started the first hotel in Nepal! I was born several years
later, in 1956, the eldest of two sons.

Although I was born into a Christian family we were

under no illusions about "inheriting" the faith. At the age of sixteen I made a decision to follow Christ, and this commitment has deepened over the years. Eventually, I felt called as an evangelist. Along with staying active in a local church in Kathmandu, that has meant leading teams into the mountains, telling people in the villages about Christ, and taking in literature and Bibles.

Nepal is officially a Hindu kingdom, the only one in the world, and we face serious legal barriers to practicing the faith. It is not technically illegal to *be* a Christian, but it is against the law to *become* a Christian or to try to persuade another person to convert to Christianity. This, of course, poses problems for an evangelist. Moreover, even if someone tries to be a silent Christian and makes no effort to tell the good news of Christ to his neighbors, he can still find himself in serious legal trouble.

Penalties can be severe for any Christian prosecuted for violating the law. A Hindu convicted of becoming a Christian will be sentenced to one year in jail. After release his conversion is legally nullified, so that if he goes into a church he is subject to reprosecution on the same charge. The penalty for attempting to *preach* Christianity is three years. And for preaching and causing a disturbance the sentence is six years.

Christians have a particularly hard time sorting out their situation in Nepal because they are loyal to the King and the royal family. There are no revolutionaries among us, and we demonstrate our loyalty in every way we can. For example, we include a picture of the King and the royal family in much of the literature we print. We do this even though we often suffer at the hands of the government.

Most of us who are active in the ministry come to know the police and the court system quite well. My first encounter took place in 1980. One of our boys was arrested while distributing literature, and I went to the police station to try to get him out. Until that time we had been able to get out of legal scrapes by using the influence of friends. As I expected, I was able to get the young man released. After he left I spent some time sitting in the station talking to a young inspector who identified himself as a Communist. As I rose to leave, I said, "I guess I'd better be going now. See you later."

"I'm sorry," he replied. "You can't leave. You're under arrest."

"On what charge?" I asked, greatly surprised.

"Well, can you deny that you preach Christianity?"

"No, I can't."

"Well, you are under arrest for preaching Christianity."

"You must be joking—you don't have any evidence."

"Yes, I have evidence. You can't deny it."

As a new officer, he wanted to demonstrate his competence and toughness by cracking down on Christians in Kathmandu. So he issued an arrest warrant in my name and called in the public prosecutor.

After we filed into the interrogation room, the public prosecutor said he didn't want to go through with the process. If I would just give them a statement denying I was a Christian and that I wouldn't preach Christianity, they would let me go free.

"I'm sorry," I said. "I can't do that."

"Well, then," replied the prosecutor, "if you'll just give me an oral statement you can walk out of here a free man."

"It would be wrong for me even to make an oral statement like that, since I have to be obedient to God."

"All right, then," he concluded reluctantly. "We'll just have to go through with it."

So they took me to the court and registered the case against me.

By late afternoon I was in a jail cell, and nobody at home or in the church knew anything about it. Finally, some of our boys realized that I was missing and that I had been at the police station that morning. They put two and two together, made some phone calls, and by

9 P.M. I was back home. It wasn't that the legal system protected me. Rather, family contacts with people of influence got me out. I had to report to the police station every day for the next two weeks, but at least I was free.

After fourteen days, the police presented the case to the court and I was freed on bail. In Nepal bail is set depending on the maximum sentence for the alleged offense. At that time bail was 540 rupees for each year of possible sentence. Since the sentence for preaching Christianity is six years, bail was set at 3,240 rupees (540 rupees for each year), which was worth about 150 American dollars. Since then they have raised the bail drastically, which is causing much hardship. Bail is now set at 9,125 rupees for each year of potential sentence.

To understand what happens in these cases, you need to know something about our judicial system. In Nepal we don't have jury trials. The case is tried before a single judge. In case of appeal, the case is heard by two judges. If an appeal is made to the supreme court, three judges hear the case. There is no separation of powers, except in theory. The government selects the judges, who are government officials responsible to other officials.

Although it was true that I was preaching Christianity in the villages and distributing literature, the police brought in false witnesses—police officers—who swore they had seen me doing it. The irony is that I had been doing what they accused me of doing, but the witnesses who said they had seen it were lying. It's common for the state to use false witnesses in these cases, and it's almost certain that the prosecutor knew the witnesses were lying.

This was a very difficult charge to beat. But my lawyer, who has been of great help to us, noticed that the statute prohibited preaching Christianity *and causing a disturbance to Hinduism.* He argued before the court that while I didn't deny preaching Christianity, there had been no public disturbance; I was innocent of any crime.

After a long, drawn-out process lasting about a year, I was finally acquitted.

In August 1983 the government began a strong anti-Christian campaign in the Kathmandu Valley. The pastor of our church, Nicanor Tamang—who is also my brother-in-law and who has since been driven out of the country—was arrested along with one of our deacons. One day during this campaign a policeman stopped me while I drove on one of the city streets. He said the chief wanted to see me. I drove to the police station and walked into the chief's office. He said, "If it was anyone else we wouldn't bother with this, but here's your arrest warrant. You're under arrest." They're always supposed to show you a warrant, but not many in Nepal know enough to ask for their rights.

I said, "What's the charge this time?"

"What else? Preaching Christianity, of course."

"Can I at least go home and get rid of my tie and pen?" They take everything away from you that you might use to harm yourself.

"All right. We'll send a police escort with you."

When I got to the house, I changed clothes and said goodbye to my wife and mother. They arrested a close associate at the same time, put us in separate jails, and tried to get us to inform on the other. They also told us fabricated stories that the other was supposed to have said. Neither of us was fooled by that tactic. We stayed calm all through the process, taking refuge in the biblical teaching that when we appeared before the king we should not worry since we would be given the words to speak.

The hard part for me was the threat that I would go for years without seeing my children. Technically, first degree criminals (our classification under the law) are not allowed to receive visitors. My second son was two years old then, and they said that when I got out of prison he would be eight and wouldn't remember me.

After the separate questioning proved fruitless, they

put my friend and me in the same cell. We had been able to take a Bible in the cell without the jailers finding out and we had regular devotions, which went a long way toward sustaining us. We were never physically beaten, although that is not unknown in Nepalese jails. Our jailers did, however, apply much mental pressure. They woke us up for interrogation in the middle of the night and made it hard for us to keep our mental balance.

The cell measured about eight feet wide by twenty feet long and held up to fifteen people at one time. A hole for urination was provided in one corner of the mud floor. There were no windows, and the air was foul. Once a day (sometimes twice) they led us out individually to a hole in the ground for defecation. If anyone had diarrhea he suffered; so did his cellmates. All manner of insects plagued us, and one night I woke up, sensing a thud, and saw a huge rat scampering across the cell.

Our cellmates had committed a variety of crimes, including theft, rape, and murder. We received no food. Anything to be eaten had to be brought in by the families of the prisoners.

One day my wife, who was to bring food for my friend and me, failed to show up. About 4:30 P.M. my mother came in tears and said, "They arrested Susan this morning." This was especially hard on me because my wife was four months pregnant with our third son. They had arrested her along with Elizabeth, her sister and the wife of our pastor. Fourteen days later they released all of us. The women were not charged with preaching, but rather were jailed on the absurdity that they had falsified their citizenship. (Their family has been in Nepal for centuries.)

Although my friend and I had been released, the charge against us was not dismissed. Legal proceedings dragged on for the next two years. Finally we were acquitted of the charge because no one could show any disturbance as the result of our preaching. But during the same trial, two of our people were convicted of converting to Christianity and were sentenced to three months. Our lawyer has appealed that conviction, but the government has appealed our acquittal. These cases are still pending. (There is no prohibition against double jeopardy in Nepal. Either side can appeal.)

Sometimes it worked to claim that we caused no disturbance, but other times it didn't. The government's role in the cases became clear just a week later when a similar case was tried. The charge was again preaching Christianity; the trial was held in the same court, with the same prosecutor, same judge, same defense attorney, and the same argument. The only difference was that the prosecution had weaker evidence against the defendant than in my case. Yet the defendant was found guilty. What must have happened is that the government, surprised by my defense, was ready by the time of the next case and instructed the judge to ignore the defense argument.

Although in all these cases we must think a great deal about legal issues, we believe the heart of the matter is spiritual. While we're in jail, the church is praying for us. We are not fighting a physical battle; it's a spiritual warfare. The Acts of the Apostles didn't end in the first century but is continuing today. We depend on the Lord's miracles for our salvation and our victory in these struggles.

We have also tried to engage Christians in the West to act on our behalf. We ask them to pray for us and to engage in letter-writing campaigns. No foreign organizations work for the Christians in Nepal, but we have contacts with individuals here and there. Through the grapevine they get out the word about what is happening to the Christians in our country.

We have found that foreign pressure works mainly in Kathmandu because that's all most foreigners know about Nepal. Even when pressure eases in the capital it's still serious in the countryside. Communications are bad in mountainous areas, which means most of Nepal. Often we in Kathmandu don't learn about persecution until long after the fact, and sometimes never. So it's much harder for foreigners to learn about and have an effect on behalf of Christians in the outlying regions.

Sometimes the government responds to complaints about persecution by denying it exists. In this they're helped by the presence of the United Mission to Nepal (UMN), which has the sanction of the Nepalese government. This mission is sponsored by a number of foreign churches and mission agencies and runs clinics, hospitals, and other humanitarian projects. The government's position is that since this missionary group functions with the approval of the Nepalese authorities, it can't be said that religious freedom doesn't exist. But UMN is allowed to function purely as a humanitarian organization; it cannot preach the gospel or represent Christ in any visible way.

For example, if you walk through the UMN hospital in Kathmandu you will not be able to find a cross, a picture, or a poster that would show it is a Christian mission station. The mission is pretty well cut off from the life of the church, which for the most part does not recognize the institution as a part of the body of Christ. (Of course, this does not deny that there are many fine believers in the mission who *are* members of the body of Christ.) If Nepalese Christians carried out their faith in that way, we would not be thrown in jail and discriminated against. But in that case, the church in Nepal would be something much less than the New Testament model it is trying to be.

We have learned to bear the constant pressure without allowing it to keep us from our task. We carry on in our responsibilities for the church and for evangelizing the people of our country. The jailings, the court cases, the darkness and terrors of the surrounding idol worship must not be allowed to distract us from our task of serving the Lord where he has placed us. [1]

Notes

1. In September 1989 the Supreme Court of Nepal confirmed the lower court's sentence of Charles Mendies to six years imprisonment, and he was arrested on November 16. As this is written he is serving his sentence in Kathmandu's central prison. His imprisonment coincided with a renewed persecution of Christians, including jailings, beatings, and raids on churches.

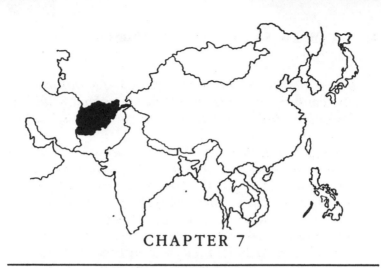

CHAPTER 7

ALONE IN AN
ISLAMIC SEA
by Ayub Zahir

Introduction: Afghanistan, a mountainous
country of central Asia, has become known to the
West in the last decade or so chiefly because of
the war between the Communist government,
assisted by Soviet forces, and the various factions
of armed guerrillas seeking to reestablish an
independent state free of communist influence.
The USSR has completed its withdrawal from
Afghanistan after failing in its intention to crush
the opposition. Most observers predicted a short
life for the puppet regime left behind, but those
expectations have been thwarted, as the civil war
takes on the appearance of a stalemate. Nobody
knows whether real peace will come any time
soon.

Despite these uncertainties, there is nothing on
the horizon that appears to hold out an end to the

*persecution suffered by Christians in Afghanistan.
The country's struggles are between communism
and Islam, both of which are hostile to Christian
faith.*

*Ayub Zahir's hard experiences came from
Islam, the likely successor to Marxism as the
philosophy that guides the state. As Marxist
influence recedes, along with the foreign army
that sustained it, the few Christians in
Afghanistan can expect increasing pressure. It
may be that if hostilities end with an Islamic
victory, things will become much harder for the
followers of Christ in Afghanistan.*

*The penalty in Afghanistan for leaving Islam is
death, although the authorities sometimes turn a
blind eye to the presence of Christians. Not
surprisingly there is no official church in the
country, apart from fellowships established by
foreigners for themselves. The few Christians that
meet together gather secretly in homes.*

• • •

I grew up in a Moslem family with six children. Our
family is middle class, and we have valued education
highly. All of us children received good educations. In
our family only my mother is illiterate. My sisters are
teachers, and my father and brothers are farmers.

My wife, Gulnar, and I have three daughters, ages
eight, six, and four. Our house is furnished very simply,
as are most in Afghanistan. *Dari*, which is a kind of floor
matting, covers the floors. We have a rather strict
separation of the sexes in our society, so that men and
women have separate areas of the house. Women usually
cannot enter where men are seated and entertained. In
the same way the women have complete privacy, and
men cannot intrude there.

I became a Christian in spite of my hostility to the

followers of Christ. As a religious leader in one of our mosques, I learned about a missionary who was "misleading" the people by teaching them from the Bible. I decided to read the Bible for myself in order to develop a strategy for attacking what he was doing by discovering the weak points. This study continued for more than two years.

It was the prophecies about Christ in the Old Testament that bothered me most about this study. Moslems believe that the Jews altered the Old Testament to cut out the prophecies about Mohammed, but if that is so, why didn't they do the same with the prophecies of Christ? I went to the synagogue to find out if the Jewish Bible was the same as the one the Christians use. I discussed this issue for days with the head of the synagogue, and had many arguments with him. Finally I came to the conclusion that the Hebrew Bible and the Old Testament that the Christians use were the same. As I continued studying, the claims of Islam concerning biblical prophecies of Mohammed looked increasingly doubtful to me. And I could find no evidence that the Bible had been changed to serve Christian ends rather than Moslem.

Coming to this point put me in a very difficult position. I was a leader of the mosque and had come to believe that the gospel of Jesus Christ—which we had always been taught to regard as the enemy of our religion—was the truth. I prayed much about this. One evening, after much prayer, it came to me that all the world's medicines would not prolong my life past one hundred years, and that was but a minute compared with the sacrifice of eternity if I allowed my natural feelings to direct my course. So I made the decision to follow Christ.

Moreover, I did not keep the decision secret, but let people know what I had done. There was immediate opposition from family, friends, and indeed from the whole society. I tried to avoid walking on the street, because people sometimes threw stones at me. The difficulties my decision brought to me made me wonder if I had made a mistake. In prayer I asked the Lord to show me in a dream whether I had allowed false teaching to lead me astray or whether I had indeed followed the way of the Almighty. There followed a series of dreams which I took to be answers to that prayer.

In the first dream I was a student in a class. The teacher was giving a lecture and students were asking questions, which I was answering. It was a Bible class. The second dream came the same night. There was a very large green field which was thronged with thousands of people. I was among the crowd, and all of us were worshiping a dove. I was very worried when I awakened, thinking to myself, "How can I worship a bird?" Falling asleep again, I had the third dream. I saw myself lying on my bed in the middle of a crossroad, greatly worried that a car would come by and hit me. A lady came and took me by the hand. She took me across the road and put me on a platform. Then she said, "Now your way is straight, just go right ahead."

"What is this place?" I wanted to know.

She replied, "This is Jerusalem."

"Who are you?"

She answered, "I am Mary, the mother of Jesus."

I awoke again. Unable to get back to sleep, I rose from my bed and tried to make sense of the dreams. It seemed to me that the scene in which I was a member of the class meant that I was to be a learner. The second dream meant that I was to worship the Holy Spirit, represented by the dove. And the third dream meant that my destination was to be the New Jerusalem. I didn't know much about it at that time, so weak was my knowledge of the New Testament. But I understood that my help would come from Jesus Christ himself. This convinced me that God approved what I had done. Ever since then I have been able to follow Christ without doubt or hesitation.

But the pressures of family and friends became no easier. My family continued to make things difficult, although off and on they seemed to accept me. Sometimes acquaintances offered me their women as a means to get me to renounce faith in Christ. Others offered material advantages. I believe all these efforts were the temptation of Satan. By the grace of God I was able to refuse them all.

Four years after my conversion Gulnar came in contact with the gospel for the first time. She didn't want to accept it, but one day when she had seen a vision of Christ the Lord crucified on a cross, she was touched and came to trust him. Only her brother knew about this because he, too, was a secret Christian. Eventually, someone found out about her faith and told her father about it. He was very angry and expelled both brother and sister from the house. The two lived together elsewhere. During the family crisis, her faith was strengthened and she was baptized.

By this time we had met and had become convinced that we should marry. She was about seven years younger than I was. I was somewhat hesitant because she was not an educated woman, and this made her unacceptable to my family. My brothers had all taken educated wives. This was somewhat embarrassing to me at first, but once I realized that it was a question of obeying the will of God I put those hesitancies behind me. The Lord was gracious to us, and my family came to accept Gulnar. Both of us have much to be thankful for despite the difficulties with our families. Their rejection could have been complete, as is often the case with Christian believers.

The number of Christians in Afghanistan is very small. Some hold government posts, but they are given a very difficult time because they are thought to be instruments of foreign intelligence organizations like the CIA—a baseless charge. I think it unlikely that those who make such charges really believe them. Rather, they use such statements in order to get at Christians. Private employers are seldom willing to hire Christians because of their hatred for anyone outside Islam. Any worker who becomes known as a Christian will almost certainly lose his job. Christians who have regular work are almost always secret believers. It is very hard for the others to support themselves. Some sell their possessions to sustain life. The authorities often fine them, which makes it even harder.

Those inclined to persecute are especially prejudiced against converted Moslems. One man said to me that they would continue their *jihad* [holy war] against Communists and Christians—both of whom they consider to be unbelievers. In the areas that follow the Ayatollah Khomeini, Christians are being killed as well as subjected to unspeakable humiliation and torture. This is all legitimate under Moslem law. Christians suffer these things much more than do Communists. But the Lord is keeping his people, and there are Moslems coming to Christ even in the midst of those horrors. The official punishment for converting is what we call *sangsar—* stoning. Some have left Afghanistan in order to practice their faith openly.

When somebody is imprisoned for his faith or suffers some other punishment, family and friends are shamed. The problem is as much social and political as religious. People in our country do not believe religion concerns only the individual. Whoever leaves Islam is thought to have rebelled against his whole society, repudiating everyone to whom he was related by blood or by friendship.

Families with children face great difficulty because no Christian schools are permitted. Parents must send their children to Moslem schools and that means they receive Islamic instruction. But many Christian families have textbooks at home which cover the same subjects from a Christian point of view, and these parents spend much time instructing their children. In grade nine, for example, when the official schools teach about marriage and family relationships, we make certain that our children learn the truth from us.

When an Afghan Christian is sent to prison his family falls into serious jeopardy. When I was in prison we understood that my wife might be arrested and tortured. The whole family is vulnerable. This contradicts the law, which says that each person is responsible for his own crime. But the state acts that way in order to make the prisoner confess; if he doesn't, they threaten his family. Even when the prisoner's family is left in peace, the separation causes great hardship. My first imprisonment lasted a year, and I saw my family only once during that period. During the second imprisonment, I was deprived of any news of my family. I did not even know if they were alive. Prison authorities threatened to arrest my wife, brother, and father if I did not confess to the charges.

Out of necessity, Christians in our society remain largely out of sight, doing what they can to blend in. This leads to difficult compromises. Most of us take part in the Moslem festivals such as Ashura, which celebrates Mohammed's birthday.

During other holidays, like Eid-i-Qurban and Eid-i-Ramadan, we decorate the house and have special foods. It is too dangerous not to do such things, but Christians who participate must consciously train themselves to feel right about it. Lately I have been thinking of the test to which I will be put if we have a boy. Moslem teachings require circumcision, and we would be under great pressure to comply.

We still have much to learn of what it means to live the Christian life in such hard circumstances. And yet there are great opportunities. In the Pakistani city of Banu, for example, one Christian student created a great stir. She was part of a group of nineteen students in an economics course. At examination time, supervised by government inspectors, all the other students were cheating. When supervisors asked her why she was not copying from her notebook like the others, she replied, *Mera Khuda Zinda Khuda Hai*—"My Lord is a Living God." This made an impact on the whole college, and indeed in the city many spoke of how Christians behave themselves.

MIDDLE EAST
AND AFRICA

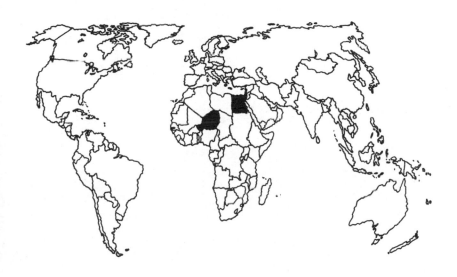

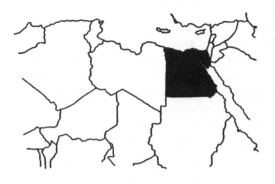

CHAPTER 8

STUDY THE BIBLE,
GO TO JAIL
by Aljabar Burani

*Introduction: North Africa has been almost
solidly Moslem for many centuries, so much so
that throughout most of the region it is extremely
hazardous for anyone to be a Christian, with the
exception of foreigners. This includes Morocco,
the homeland of Aljabar Burani. In Egypt,
however, a legal Christian community dates back
to about the beginning of the Christian church.
By the time Islam began in the seventh century,
Christianity was the religion of Egypt. But the
militant Islamic onslaught soon changed that,
and Islam became the main religion in the area
by force of arms. Christianity has been on the
defensive ever since, with periods of intense
persecutions alternating with periods of relatively
mild treatment.*

Since Christianity is a legal term in Egypt,

defining not so much religious belief as communal membership, the intensity and sincerity of Christian commitment varies widely. Emigration is high among Egyptian Christians, and so is conversion to Islam, usually under pressure of marriage ties or because of opportunities for career advancement. An estimated 18 percent of the population professes Christianity, down about 1 percent since 1900. All but a very small percentage are members of the Coptic Church, an eastern orthodox communion.

As in other Moslem countries, the religious situation is complicated by the hostilities of the Middle East. The Islamic revolution in Iran bred widespread, militant hostility to any country friendly to Israel or to any religion besides Islam. The Islamic Brotherhood—the group responsible for President Sadat's assassination in 1981—is strong in many places. This not only makes it difficult for Christians to profess their faith, but makes it difficult for the government to pursue policies that are not one-sidedly pro-Islam. Making things much more sensitive is the general hostility to Israel throughout the Arab world, which transforms otherwise simple decisions into high-risk propositions. No doubt this is part of the reason the Egyptian government kept Mr. Burani in prison for so long, despite the damage this caused to its reputation.

Christians are undergoing much harassment in Egypt even as this is written. Discrimination in education and employment occur every day. Some languish in prison. Churches are being burned. Still, in the North African context, Christians have it better in Egypt than anywhere else. That is why Mr. Burani went to Cairo in the first place. The training he sought there would have been impossible to find in his native Morocco, because the police would have closed it down immediately and meted out severe punishment to all participants.

• • •

I am a Moroccan by birth and upbringing. I heard the gospel when I was a child through contact with missionaries. The religion of Morocco is Islam, and it is very difficult to be a Christian there. Everyone knows that to be Moroccan is to be a Moslem, so if someone says he is a Christian it is nearly incomprehensible. It sounds impossible. Unlike others I was never persecuted in Morocco because I never told anyone I was a Christian.

But I know many who had trouble with the police because of their faith. In one incident in 1976 or 1977, some of our group talked about Christ to friends at work. The friends called the police, who came and questioned our people. One of them gave out the names of everyone in our group. Almost everybody was called to the police station for questioning. I was very young then (about fifteen) and that is probably why the police did not come to my house. At the time I was not even a believer, just searching for the truth.

Another time neighbors reported a Christian who did not take part in a mandatory Islamic fast. The police questioned him, and he admitted he did not fast because he was a Christian. His lawyer told him he should lie and deny being a Christian but he refused to do so; he spent six months in prison. There are many examples like that. The cost of following Christ in Morocco is high.

At the same time we often find that when the persecution gets bad, the church grows more. Sometimes when persecution breaks out in Casablanca people come to Christ elsewhere in the country. In that sense persecution can be a blessing.

We have learned not to compare ourselves with

others. Believers have blessings in New York that we do not have, but the opposite is also true. If we make comparisons between each other we lose sight of God's differing calls and his various blessings for his people.

My personal introduction to persecution came in Egypt. I met a foreign believer in Morocco who told me about a Christian conference called Explo 85. Numerous messages were to be given from around the world and transmitted by satellite. I went to the meeting in Cairo along with about ten brothers and sisters from Morocco. We learned many things we had not known. For the first time I was in a regular church. I learned about witnessing, discipleship, and many basic things that every Christian should know. For the first time I experienced what it means to be part of the worldwide body of Christ. After this I went back to Morocco and finished my studies. The next year I had some time off and returned to Egypt for more training, this time in Alexandria.

When a brother from Morocco and I arrived in Egypt, we received our training with two Tunisians. The four of us lived together in an apartment in Alexandria. This was a very exciting time. The trouble started when we went to the police station to extend our visas. They wanted to know more about our status. We were supposed to be in Egypt as tourists, not workers or students. So they wanted to know how we were living, where our money came from, how we could keep the apartment. There were many difficult questions. Everything we were doing was legal, but the officials did not try to hide their hostility.

Our ordeal began one night when the Tunisians did not return to the apartment. Waiting up late for them, I decided to call our ministry director to see if he knew anything about their whereabouts. As I picked up the telephone three men burst into the room. One of them yelled, "Who are you talking to?"

"I was calling a friend," I replied, startled. They were policemen in civilian clothing, and one of our Tunisian

friends was with them. He looked very frightened, and
we learned later that he had endured many hours of
questioning. The policemen woke up my sleeping
Moroccan friend, Ali, and one of them yelled at him:
"Don't you receive guests in your home?" They saw all
the Christian books and papers, including the schedule of
the training program, and stuffed them into suitcases. A
gold chain belonging to one of us also disappeared into
the pocket of one of the officers. It was about 11 P.M.

For two days and nights they would not let us sleep.
They gave us nothing to eat. Finally, one policeman took
some money we gave him and brought back a sandwich
for each of us. There were always three or four people
asking us questions. They did not act rationally, but
raved at us because they knew everything we were
doing. We could tell they had known about us for some
time and probably had followed us around. They knew
the names of those who had visited us. We believe that
some of their informants were among our guests in the
apartment.

I had an appointment with my Bible study leader the
next day to show him my lesson. But when he came for
the meeting the police arrested him also and brought him
in. They gave us all beatings: the Egyptian leader, the
two Tunisians, and us two Moroccans. They asked a
question, and if they did not like the answer they would
strike us with an open hand across the face. Sometimes
they gave us the answer first, and then asked the
question; if we gave any answer but the one they
expected they struck us.

"What do you think of Christians?" an officer would
ask.

"They are nice people."

"Are you saying Moslems are bad?" and *bang* would
come a police hand across the face.

The questioning was very clever. They already knew
most of the answers before they asked, so they were
testing us to see if we would lie. Also they were trying to

break us down psychologically with the procedures—the hostility, the hunger, and sleeplessness.

"Why are you here?"

"To study the Bible."

"Why don't you stay in your own country to study the Bible?"

"Because it isn't allowed."

"If you can't study the Bible in your own country, you can't study it in mine. What is your goal in Egypt?"

"To be able to understand what is in the Bible."

"So you can evangelize Moslems in Cairo?"

"No. Most of the people I know in Egypt are already Christians."

Besides questions about Christianity, they also asked about Islam and politics. When they showed us books from our apartment against Islam, I was able to show them additional books against Christianity. I think they were making things uncomfortable for us so that we would hate Christianity, associating our faith with the treatment we were receiving.

They accused us of many things which they had no reason to believe. We think this was done to break us down psychologically. They made us take off all our clothes and stand naked before them while they asked questions about our sexual lives. They accused us of being homosexuals. They kept asking how we could be Christians when we had Moslem names. They were very sarcastic and said we were betraying our family, our tradition, and our country. They accused us of being paid by outsiders to harm Egypt by causing riots. They said we were trying to turn Egypt into another Lebanon with its civil war along communal lines. The questioning was accompanied by continual slaps on the face and much kicking.

The cell crowding was extremely bad. We were compressed with many other prisoners into a tiny space, heads bowed down, and wearing handcuffs. The odor gagged us. We spent one night in a cave beneath the police station.

After three days of questioning we were taken from the jail in Alexandria to a political prison outside Cairo—Torah Prison, where they had taken the men who killed President Sadat. This was a dangerous place for us; Sadat had been killed by the Moslem Brotherhood because they thought he was not ruling for the benefit of Islam. The Brotherhood has a special hatred for Christians, especially for those who convert from Islam.

The authorities continued to question us at the prison, but now the questioning grew harder. They hated us. We could tell it by the way they acted, but also they told us about it frankly.

They beat us on the soles of our feet with a stick and then made us run in place, so that we thought our feet would explode with pain. There were also blows on the ribs with a stick. They told me to write down the names of the books they had confiscated from the apartment. For each one I could not remember there was another whack with the stick. They humiliated us further by cutting our hair on one side and leaving the other long.

The police put an informer in the cell with us. He asked so many questions, including some the police had asked, that it was easy to tell what he was doing. They also put a convert to Islam in with us to urge us to convert. Our Tunisian comrades were worse off than we were. They landed in a cell with a dozen sheiks of the Moslem Brotherhood! This was a terrifying experience, and they easily could have been killed.

We learned later that our friends in Cairo did not know for two months where we were. They reported our disappearance to the police who told them we had returned to Morocco. The prison authorities refused to send a letter out of the prison for us, but we eventually found a guard who could be bribed. They took all our money when we entered the prison, but through a Christian brother among the prisoners we got enough money to give to the guard. Our friends on the outside learned where we were through the letter he mailed.

Prison life was hard. They squeezed us together in tiny, dark cells where the air was stale and swarming with flies and mosquitoes. For the first two months we could not shave, bathe, or brush our teeth. There was little food—just beans and rice—and it was filthy and full of worms and other insects. After delaying as long as I could, I asked the Lord to help me eat. Fingering the beans, I picked out a worm and flung it away. Then I crouched in a dark corner where I could not see the food and stuffed it in my mouth, handful by handful. Drinking water was contaminated by the hole in the floor that served as our toilet. We had nothing at all to do except to stare at the four walls. The cell contained neither chair nor bed. We slept on the stone floor.

Prisoners were permitted to buy food in the canteen with an account drawn from cash they had brought with them. In order to do that you had to bribe the guards with cigarettes. But our guards wouldn't accept anything from us because it was known we had abandoned Islam and were thus unclean.

The sheiks took it upon themselves to convert us back to Islam. They appointed one of their number named Mamoud to do this, and he pursued us relentlessly. He bombarded us with quotes from the Koran and misquotes from the Bible. He even sent an illiterate prisoner to ask us to read aloud a newspaper article. It turned out to be a call for death to apostates from Islam. The article ended by rejoicing that some already had been rounded up.

Mamoud kept changing his tactics—one day raging at us, the next being kind and gentle. Once he surprised one of the Tunisians by asking how he became a Christian, and when our friend told him, he erupted in anger and ordered him out of the cell.

All this added greatly to our depression, and we started to lose hope. We felt as if we were undergoing a slow descent toward death, as if we were dying one bit at a time. Our morale kept sinking until we began to pray together and recite Bible verses. This became the best medicine for our mental state. We were cheered when we kept in mind Hebrews 13:5, which says that Christ would never fail us nor forsake us. We meditated on the sufferings of Christ and the early church, and considered Bible passages showing how they rejoiced even in the midst of suffering. We became bolder and sang out together. While we sang the sheik loudly read out of the Koran to compete with us.

As we learned how to rejoice in our terrible circumstances, our spiritual state improved. We were always blaming someone for what happened to us, either ourselves or others. And we allowed ourselves to sink into self-pity. "What have I done to deserve this?" Now we stopped blaming ourselves and recognized that suffering is normal for a follower of Christ. As we accepted our situation we learned to accept other things also, such as the food.

One day we faintly heard a Christian program on someone's radio. After much effort and over a long period of time we were able to persuade a guard to buy a radio for us in the canteen. Regularly hearing Christian broadcasts from Trans World Radio in Monte Carlo was a great comfort to us.

After three months we learned that one of our fellow prisoners was a Christian. He was less confined than we were and he brought us extra food and a New Testament. We discovered ways in which to keep the numerous surprise searches from uncovering the Testament.

After our friends on the outside discovered where we were they began praying for us. By that time we had only the remnants of the clothes we wore when the police brought us in, so our friends sent us clothing. They sent food too, but none of it reached us.

One day a guard brought us out to a large room where a man in a dark business suit awaited us. "I am your lawyer," he said. "Your brothers in France and

Germany have hired me to represent you." We were immediately suspicious because we didn't know anyone in France or Germany. In answer to our question he laughed and admitted that he was Moslem, not Christian. But he had been well paid to take this case, one that no other lawyer would touch. He assured us that he would have us out of prison before long.

Two weeks later we found ourselves in court, in a cage behind bars along with the defendants of seven other cases. The lawyer's assistant was there. When the time came for our case, we were taken to another room away from public scrutiny. The prosecutor told the court that we were caught defaming Islam and proselytizing for Christianity. He also reported that we were Moslems who had converted. Our lawyer's assistant denied the charges and said that everything we had done was legal. He pointed out that our books were not only legal but also approved by the Council of Churches in Egypt, and that he would be glad to produce a letter from the Council to that effect.

Nobody spoke to us at the hearing, and the whole thing probably took no more than five or six minutes. The judge quickly pronounced his judgment: our imprisonment would continue. This was a crushing blow to us. But we did learn that we should have trusted the Lord rather than the lawyer.

After this "trial" our treatment improved. Our lawyer persuaded prison officials to allow us out of our cells for six hours a day. We could shave, shower, and brush our teeth. Our lawyer brought pajamas and food, and he put money into our accounts at the canteen. The guards began honoring our requests to buy food and newspapers.

Some time later we appeared in court a second time and once more were put into the cage. A lawyer showed up and asked where the backsliders were. When we identified ourselves he said that if we would confess Islam right then he would defend us free of charge and would guarantee our immediate release. We declined.

In September we were again brought into court, now in closed session with no other prisoners present. This time our lawyer himself was there, and before a different judge. The prosecutor read the allegations. He was exceedingly harsh, trying to convince the judge that we were professional rioters who had come to destroy the country, to dissolve it in the same way Lebanon was being destroyed.

Our lawyer made two points in his rebuttal. The first was that Egypt had signed international agreements to honor freedom of belief for all people, including foreigners living in the country. Second, he said the world already knew that Egypt was not honoring her commitments. He read an article from a French newspaper to demonstrate this. He also read passages from the constitutions of Egypt, Tunisia, and Morocco, all of which guarantee freedom of religion. He affirmed his own Islamic faith and the fact that he did not believe as we did, but said that this kind of consideration was irrelevant in judging our case.

The prosecution cited Islamic law, under which we should be put to death as apostates. Our lawyer replied that the Koran does not so stipulate. He said that only "hypocrites" were to be put to death—defined as those who had converted to Islam and then reverted to their former religion. Therefore he concluded that by any standard of law—international, constitutional, or Islamic—we had been illegally arrested and imprisoned. He also charged that the police had brutalized us illegally. And he pointed out the damage that had been done to Egypt's international reputation by this case.

It had been a stirring defense, and the judge was clearly troubled. Still, we had learned by our ordeal not to trust in human justice. The judge ordered us and our lawyer to leave the room while he consulted with his advisors. After a time an official came out and handed a piece of paper to the lawyer. His face darkened as he read it. "Continuation of imprisonment until further notice."

So back to the cells we went. We were taken on a public bus, handcuffed together. The guards pushed us constantly and humiliated us. One policeman shouted at the top of his voice, "You move and I'll shoot."

Despite all this, our faith in the Lord's provision grew stronger than ever. But now conditions again worsened. We were only allowed outside the cells for one daily run to the toilet. Our canteen privileges were canceled, and we were back to eating wormy beans and rice. We did receive one blessing in the midst of all the bad news: Sheik Mahmoud departed to another part of the prison, and we were spared his preaching and hatred.

We had worked the Egyptian legal system as hard as we knew how, and it proved unable to provide justice. But just then the international scene became active. As word spread of our imprisonment, pressure increased on the government to release us. Many letters came from outside the country. Amnesty International declared us to be prisoners of conscience. Two Christian congressmen from the United States wrote to the Egyptian ambassador in Washington. So now the case was out of the hands of the court and in the hands of the government. It was all political. But pressure from the outside made things happen. One day as we were lying around the cell the guards came to release us. We were to be taken to the deportation center and expelled from the country.

At the deportation center we realized that our problems were not over. If we returned home to Tunisia and Morocco, what would happen there? Those countries do not have a legal Christian community, as does Egypt. Would we be moving from the frying pan into the fire? We bribed a guard to look the other way while we used a telephone to call a friend. The wheels began grinding again, but one country after the other refused to accept us. Finally, on November 4, we were driven to the Cairo airport, put on an Air France plane, and pushed into seats. Our handcuffs were removed, and we were on the way to our new home in France.

We learned a great deal from our time in prison. God was with us. We learned to pray, and prayer was food to us. We learned to love and forgive even those who put us in prison. We learned what liberty means. In Christ we were free—even in prison—because we learned to have no desire for sin. And we learned to be free when we had nothing.

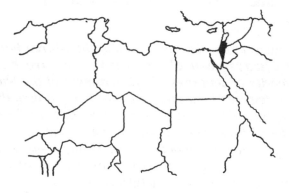

CHAPTER 9

STANDING UP TO THE YAD L'ACHIM

by Kenneth Crowell

Introduction: The small republic of Israel, in existence only some forty years, is situated at the eastern end of the Mediterranean Sea, near the crossroads of Europe, Asia and Africa. The country was born of the determination of millions of Jews from all over the world following the massacre of some six million of their people during the brief Nazi domination of Europe. They aimed to build a Jewish homeland that would serve as a sanctuary.

Although Israel was established as a Jewish state it has strong roots in the western countries in which freedom of religion had long been established. Christians have therefore suffered little or no official discrimination. The memories of the Nazi holocaust remain strong, however, and many Jews have thought that Gentile means

Christian. *Moreover, the hands of the church have not always been clean, and there are bad memories of centuries of mistreatment of the Jews by professing Christians. In the Holy Land itself the remains of Crusader structures dating from medieval times dot the landscape—some right in the very walls of the old city of Jerusalem—and no Israeli has forgotten that they represent the imposition of Christianity by force of arms.*

No consideration of modern Israel can ignore the most visible and painful source of tension in the land: the dispute between Arab and Jew. Many thousands of Arabs were displaced from their territory when the Jewish state was set up after World War II, and three bloody wars were fought over the country. Israelis are conscious of their status as an island in a sea of Arabs who would like to force them out or destroy them completely. Yet Israel itself is home to many Arabs, and some way to accommodate the legitimate rights of all its citizens will have to be found.

With the Israeli occupation of Arab lands after the 1973 war, the seeds for greater tension were sown. At the very time Kenneth Crowell prepared this chapter, Israel was exploding with violence between Arabs and Jews. The so-called intefadeh, *or uprising, which continues as this is being written, is intended to force Israel to depart from the disputed territories on the West Bank of the Jordan river and the Gaza strip.*

The decade of the eighties has seen one development of interest to Christians. Numerous small fellowships of Christians have appeared in various parts of the country that are not part of either the established western denominations or the long-standing Arab Christian community. Mr. Crowell speaks of them briefly toward the end of this chapter. Some of them consciously do not call

*themselves "Christian," but instead stress their
status as completed Jews or messianic Jews and
followers of Jesus.*

• • •

*F*rom the beginning of our time in Israel, about ten
years ago, we had two overriding motivations. We
were committed to helping build the nation by
contributing to its economic development, and we were
committed to serving Jesus Christ faithfully in that
environment. When we started, we saw no contradiction
between those two commitments and we still see none
today. We've had difficulties in the last few years with
some of our neighbors, but they don't represent the
convictions or the practices of the vast majority of the
Israeli people nor of their government.

My wife and I started out in Tel Aviv. I had gone
there as an engineer, and I found it natural to live openly
as a Christian, witnessing to the faith and giving out
Bibles and other literature to anyone who was interested.
In the evenings I held Bible studies with fellow workers.
We were well accepted and had no problems. Where
persecution is a problem in modern Israel it's due to
local circumstances and personalities and isn't a function
of national policy. Certainly the average citizen of Israel
doesn't regard us as a threat.

The problems that developed are due largely to a
group called the Yad L'Achim, which means "hand to the
brethren." This militant orthodox group is concerned
about protecting the rights of Jews but interprets that
mission in a way that most Israelis reject. Most of its
money comes from American and Canadian Jews, and in
order to keep the funds flowing it acts strongly against
what it regards as missionary activity. If it can't find
missionary activity it may falsify what it's doing to keep
donors writing checks. In other words, the Yad L'Achim
needs an enemy in order to stay in business.

We live in Tiberias, an ancient town of about forty thousand inhabitants on the western bank of the Sea of Galilee. It is considered one of the four holy cities in Israel, largely because of the extra-biblical writings and famous rabbis associated with it. Some people think that having Christians here desecrates the ancient traditions. Little open witness takes place in Tiberias.

It's hard to say what changed this situation except for a few events that seem to be coincidental. At least none of us dreamed up any master plan. As far as we can tell, a few Christians drifted in from various places. Some came from *kibbutzim*, the cooperative farm communities so common in the Israeli countryside. Some are expatriates from Europe or North America who have moved to Israel to work. Some are immigrants.

We came here to set up a company called Galtronics. We worked through the Jewish Agency regional office in Atlanta. I told them frankly that I was not Jewish, that I would be going to Israel as a Christian in order to help the nation develop economically. They knew I had worked there before and that I would not relinquish my testimony or my faith. With all this on the table, they said: "All right. Come and help us build the country, and we'll support you in the effort." They assured us that Israel had freedom of religion and there would be no problem. True to their word, within eight months we were up and running; normally we could have expected a three-year wait before the red tape could be cleared away. Our business is electronic technology with special interest in the export market, which is one reason the government wanted us to set up shop here.

When we came to Tiberias the local newspaper did a story on us and described us as a Christian company. The mayor and his staff gave us a warm welcome. Shortly after we opened for business, however, the mayor left office. The new mayor was the only religious mayor in the country and his cabinet shared his views. Israel in many respects is secular, and although several religious parties have a strong following, most politicians have not followed their wishes. Our local politicians were not typical. They opposed any Christian witness in the city.

As our business grew, we hired a number of believers. It was natural for them to meet together as a fellowship as there existed no indigenous Christian worship in the city. Gradually it dawned on people that we were more than traditional Christians, that we took our faith seriously. Some of the orthodox Jews in the city came to believe we were a problem because we accepted Jews into the fellowship, and the city's new politics did not help us.

We first felt the tension about six years ago, a full five years after we after we came to Tiberias. The church was growing strong, numbering about fifty or sixty members. The Yad L'Achim began spreading the story that we were not so much a business as a missionary society, an organization paid by outsiders to do mission work. Newspaper headlines spoke of "Messiah Galtronics." We don't fall into that category at all. Our income is completely derived from our business activities and friends who help support the work, just as we told the government. But much misinformation is circulated deliberately.

Our fellowship met in a hotel in Tiberias. One day the head of the Yad L'Achim brazenly walked in during the middle of a meeting and began snapping pictures of everyone there. He just walked up to someone, put a camera in his face, and took the picture. We asked him to leave but he refused; finally we ushered him out. Only then could we resume our meeting.

The Yad L'Achim told us they had no problem with Gentiles starting a church. The trouble was the Jewish believers among us, and they couldn't accept that at all. The next week they came back to the hotel and stood outside yelling and throwing rocks at us. The next week the same thing happened while we were having communion. They began hiring gangsters to do their work for them, and one week they threw a five-pound rock through the window that hit my wife on the head and knocked her down. A little lower and it could have killed her. They broke windows and grabbed at people inside.

By then we had asked for police protection. But the police were mixed up themselves, caught between their plain duty and the false messages coming from the Yad L'Achim. Even when we went to the police station to ask for protection the officers were divided. Someone would say, "I'm not going to help them," and a supervisor would reply, "You have to. It's your job." One time a commander who belongs to a Moslem sect called the Druze ordered his Jewish sergeant to help us, but the sergeant refused. The commander insisted and gave the sergeant a direct order to go. Finally the sergeant left, but he never showed up to help us.

Finally thugs set fire to the hotel and damaged it severely. We paid the owner for the damage and began meeting in the countryside. In the summer we meet on the side of a mountain and in the winter we rent a youth hostel away from the city. We moved the meetings to an outlying area in order not to jeopardize other people's property.

Meeting in the woods has advantages, but it doesn't put us out of reach of the Yad L'Achim. Fires have been set in the woods near our meetings. Orthodox groups of eight to ten people have stood face to face with people of our congregation. Arrogance and intimidation is the rule.

"Outlandish" is the only word for some stories about us. According to one tale, we gave tennis shoes to children in order to entice them into adopting our religious beliefs. Another rumor had us stealing children off the streets. Yet another said we were giving children chocolate candies with white crosses printed on the top. As these stories began to circulate, the newspaper printed them. None of these rumors start as misunderstandings;

they are pure fabrications intended to discredit us.

Several months ago the Yad L'Achim imported about two hundred orthodox believers. They began shouting out in city squares the names of every Christian in the city, Jew and Gentile, giving their addresses, and calling them all missionaries.

What helped us most was the good testimony of the believers. We did a lot of praying and a lot of waiting; we didn't attempt to fight back or attack anybody. Once when we went to a little candy store downtown a woman said to me: "Have you heard of the terrible things that are going on in our city? Our children are being kidnaped and brainwashed." I answered that I had heard the rumors, but that they weren't true. "How do you know it isn't true?" she asked. When I replied it was because I was one of the people so accused, she said, "No, it can't be true."

Christians in the company have also established an excellent reputation with the other employees. When we have a problem with false rumors our employees go to the news media and set the record straight. This kind of reputation has meant that when the Yad L'Achim stage a meeting downtown to denounce us, they don't have much of an audience. Once a militant group came to the company and told us frankly that they weren't having any success in turning the general populace against us.

Most of the persecution is directed against Jewish believers; Gentile Christians do not bother the Yad L'Achim. Still, the hostility spills over onto others. The doors to our houses have been painted, tires have been slashed. Someone makes a profession of faith, and upon leaving one of our meetings finds a note left on his car: "This time we cut your tires. Next time it will be worse." Attempts have been made to drive us out of the city. One man, an elder in the fellowship, has been told twice he would be killed.

There is another aspect to the thug-like treatment we receive from the Yad L'Achim. Under Israeli law it's possible for a repentant convict to be freed from prison under the care of a rabbinical group. Taking advantage of this law, the Yad L'Achim have gained the release of many prisoners and taken responsibility for them. About sixty percent of their members are ex-convicts. One of them put it this way to one of our elders: "This is more criminal than when I was a criminal. I'm getting out."

When intimidation and physical mistreatment failed to get us out, they began to use legal means. They went to the Ministry of Industry and the Ministry of Labor and wrote letters to a variety of other agencies to apply pressure on us.

When those moves failed, they went to a semi-official organization called the *Histradut*. This group sent its leaders to us and told us they were putting our company under their jurisdiction. We said we would not join. They tried to organize our workers but failed. When they couldn't recruit our employees by claiming to take their side against management, they returned to us and told us that if we would place ourselves under their jurisdiction they would take our side against the workers. "Look, I told the people out there that we're for them, but we're really for you. If you have a problem, we'll back you all the way. Just join with us." We showed them the door.

A few days later while our employees were on the way to work they heard on the radio about a strike at Galtronics. That made no sense to them. They said, "Why are we striking? We're not in a labor union." About an hour after work began that morning a truckload of about thirty-five goons hired by the Histradut drove up to the company. They marched in, pushed our people out of the way, and sat down at the machines. About fifteen orthodox from the Yad L'Achim then drove up in their black clothes and danced around outside of the factory, yelling at us.

I called the police, who sent one man down to sort things out. The Histradut leaders quickly got him off in a corner to argue with him while their comrades continued to occupy the place. Everything had collapsed into bedlam, so I told all our workers to go home; we were closing up for the day. With great effort we got the intruders out and locked up.

We pressed charges against the Histradut for minor acts of vandalism, and they countered by fabricating about thirty-five violations of the labor law. They published these violations in the newspapers and tried to bring in the Ministry of Labor against us. Meanwhile they were still trying to negotiate a contract, without success. To bring pressure against us they began talking to our bankers. They said I was leaving the country and taking with me the cash from the company's accounts, so the bank called me in and demanded that I surrender my passport. When I refused, they insisted on guarantees that I wouldn't allow the company to collapse.

The bankers had believed a story in the local newspaper that our workers were striking and they feared their whole investment would be lost. "Look," I said to them, "you guys know me. Do you really believe that we would do something like that?" But their orders came from the head office in Jerusalem, and they had no choice. Our working capital came from them, and they had the right to call it in, so I surrendered my passport.

Nevertheless, the bank's officers in Jerusalem weren't satisfied. They believed all the false reports and said that with all the labor violations and with the work force on strike, the company had no future. So I asked them, "Please, send an investigating team and find out for yourselves what's going on. Don't accept the information you're getting from elsewhere." Immediately they sent out a full audit team and investigated the company. They found everyone on the job, the books in good shape, and the company functioning normally. Our problems with the bank cleared up.

All these experiences have prompted some interesting conclusions about our fellowship. The pressures on us have made us more cohesive as a body.

We're a mixed group of Christians, about sixty percent Jewish and forty percent others. As soon as we fell under this persecution, the media let the whole country know about it.

We were encouraged when a pastor in a nearby Arab village called us and said "We have a place for you to meet." People from Nazareth, Tel Aviv, Jerusalem, and Haifa called to say, "What can we do to help? Can we stand with you?" They offered money and wanted to know what else they could do. They sent teams of their people to be with us. They came to our meetings and stood with us when rocks were thrown.

Not only did we see a drawing together of our local fellowship, but we also witnessed a unity of similar fellowships throughout the nation. These groups are only about ten years old in Israel, but in a crisis they showed their unity in the body of Christ. These incidents served as a kind of magnet pulling us all together. One of the most heartening things about it is the unity showed by Jewish and Arab believers, a testimony sorely needed in the midst of Israel's present troubles.

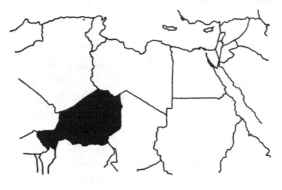

CHAPTER 10

ISLAM MAKES A "BIG CATCH"

by Christopher Shu'aibu Abashiya

Introduction: Nigeria is a former British colony on the west coast of Africa. Islam dominates in the north of the country and is numerically important in the west. It came to the region in the eleventh century. By the fifteenth century, Kano, in the far north, flourished as a center of Moslem culture.

Christianity first entered Nigeria in modern times through Methodist missionaries in 1842. By this time the fifteenth century Catholic presence had petered out. Presbyterians followed the Methodists, and after them came Baptists.

In all, some 49 percent of the population considers itself Christian; the corresponding number for Moslems is 45 percent. (These figures are disputed; evidently it is difficult to get an accurate count). Despite the fact that they are not numerically predominant, Moslems in Nigeria have acquired significant political influence, and many Christians fear that the government intends to make Islam the state religion. This is officially denied, but there is considerable reason to question the denials.

In January 1986 President Ibrahim Babangida, a Moslem, secretly enrolled Nigeria in the Organization of Islamic Conference, an act which he denied would make Islam a state religion. Many Christians think otherwise. The Christian Association of Nigeria, an organization in which Dr. Abashiya is a prominent leader, has filed suit against the federal government over the establishment of a commission that uses public money to support Moslem pilgrimages. Its argument is that the commission assists only Moslems, and this violates the federal constitution which provides for the separation of church and state.

Tensions flared into widespread violence in 1987 when some hundred and fifty churches, as well as four mosques, burned to the ground in a single day. The Christian community in Zaria was especially hard hit, with only two churches left standing out of seventy-four in use the previous day. Christian businesses and property also went up in smoke, and some believers perished. Things have been relatively quiet since then, but not many believe that the hostilities have been settled.

• • •

*T*he news of my daughter Jummai's conversion to Islam struck the public's imagination like a thunderbolt. Because I had held a variety of government and academic positions, I was well known among the Christians of Nigeria. In addition to those positions, I had occupied a variety of posts in the Christian community: I was the first Nigerian Director of the Nigerian Bible Translation Trust; for many years I have been the Chairman of the Fellowship of Christian Students; and most recently I was the sole representative of the Christian Association of Nigeria on a panel investigating the religious riots in Kaduna State in March 1987. Also I had acted as a spokesman for the Christian community, fighting against the legal establishment of Islamic law (the Sharia) when the 1979 federal constitution was being written. Taken together, all this made it seem incredible to many people that my daughter could have become a Moslem.

In order to put this into perspective, you must realize that my origins are Moslem. As a member of the Hausa-Fulani tribe, I was brought up in that faith and came to Christ as an adult. Although I had gone to missionary schools as a child, only while in post-secondary education did I decide to follow Christ. Anyone who understands Islam will recognize that my people, and indeed all Moslems, find conversions like this unacceptable. In fact, many believe the Koran requires the killing of any Moslem who accepts another religion.

I escaped death, but was forced to drink certain concoctions intended to bring about my reconversion. Moslems often write verses from the Koran on a slate, then wash the writing off with water, and force someone to drink the residue, believing that the liquid charms the one who drinks it. Sometimes they mix in certain herbs supposed to have magical qualities when incantations are said over them. These methods are not part of orthodox Islam, but result from syncretism with fetish practices (which, unfortunately, sometimes plagues Christianity as well).

This unwillingness of Moslems to see one of their number become a Christian was underscored for me during the drafting of our 1979 Constitution. I was the only Christian invited to deliver a paper at the conference. After my paper, one lecturer from the Faculty of Law in the university said to me, "Dr. Abashiya, we do not know why you are still alive. You should have been killed." "Why? What have I done?" I replied. "We know you are a Hausa-Fulani," he answered, "and born as a Moslem. The Sharia law says whoever changes from the Islamic religion to another should be killed." I tried to make a joke of the whole thing, but I could see that he was in deadly earnest. Christianity's teaching of love, even love for one's enemies, is foreign to Islam.

Just as the Christians of Nigeria were shocked by my daughter's conversion, so the Moslems were elated. One of their publications put it this way: "Islam has made a very, very big catch." We still had heard nothing from Jummai when this appeared. Then another Moslem paper carried a similar story that confirmed the report. Both publications included Jummai's picture. She had left home about three months earlier and reappeared in the home of a Moslem sheik, so I can't say the newspaper item surprised her mother and me as it did the public.

Actually, trouble had been brewing for five years before Jummai made her final break. In 1984 my cousin Kano's wife insisted that we allow Jummai to spend summer vacation with her family. We did not want this to happen because we needed her to work on the family farm. As my wife and I discussed the issue, however, I concluded that my cousin, a Moslem, would believe that it was on religious grounds that we did not allow Jummai to visit them. So we decided to permit her to stay with them for a week.

To our surprise, one week turned into three. We suspected something was wrong as soon as Jummai set foot in the house. She opened the door, saw her mother, and said, "This house smells bad." Her mother replied, "Jummai, if you feel that we and the house smell bad you can go back to Kano."

That was the beginning of a bad period for our family. Something had gone wrong with Jummai's thinking. All our efforts to counsel her failed. It was like talking to somebody who has made up his mind; nothing sinks in. We were left in no doubt as to the cause of her change. She openly told us that Kano's family had urged her to become a Moslem. When we asked how she replied, she said she told them that her parents would not approve of her conversion. But she refused to disclose to us her own thinking. We soon learned the truth anyway, because we saw in her diary that she had vowed to become a Moslem and to marry a Moslem.

This especially distressed us because it was unexpected. Unlike me, Jummai had been brought up in a Christian home. We brought her up in the fear of the Lord. Her first schools were mission schools. We had devotions in the home every day and discussed Christian faith with her and her younger brother. We prayed daily for them. We brought her up to know the truth and provided for all her physical needs and her education. That is all parents can do. Humanly speaking, I don't know of anything else we could have done. In the Hausa and Jaba language we have a saying: "You can only give birth to a child; you cannot give birth to its character."

After my own conversion I had gone through many efforts to bring me back to Islam, none of which had any impact. But my daughter had never trusted the Lord and the Islamic conversion attempts reached her. We suspect that concoction-drinking was one of the methods used on her. Our house grew tense until Jummai graduated from the College of Education at Kafanchan. We disagreed about whether she should look for a job in another city or whether we should look for employment for her near our home. She finally took matters into her own hands. One day when I returned from the farm she was gone, along with her belongings. Later we discovered she went to the house of Gumi, a Moslem, and we believe she got there with the help of one of my cousins.

The Moslem press reported that we had threatened Jummai if she converted, but that was untrue. All we told her was that salvation was to be found in Christ and not in Islam, and that she would have to face the consequences of her decision. We also told her that we could not give our blessing to her marriage with a Moslem and that we were warning her against doing such a thing. But we did not threaten her in any way.

This attitude is foreign to Moslems, as my own experience illustrates. I know of cases in which parents have threatened their children with death because they wanted to change their religion. If Moslems would permit their people to convert I believe considerable numbers would become Christians. As for the conversions of nominal Christians in the other direction, in most cases they were promised a good job, a promotion, a wife, or material benefits. But for a Moslem who becomes a Christian, the only thing promised is suffering and persecution in this world—but in the next, life everlasting.

I do not doubt the uproar that would have occurred had it been their daughter instead of ours who had changed her religion. I asked a member of the executive committee of one of the Islamic organizations to imagine what would have happened if Gumi's daughter were staying in the house of our bishop. Would Nigeria be at peace today? He agreed that it would not. Some people have asked us what we intended to do about our daughter's being in a Moslem house, and we replied, "Nothing." We don't want to do anything that might plunge the country into another religious crisis. Gumi is perfectly aware that if the tables were turned and his daughter had come to us, he would start a war.

If Gumi is so desperate to have a daughter, it is our privilege to give him one. I told my Moslem friends, "Jummai will have two homes to inherit, from Gumi and from us" (although she may not wish to inherit anything from us in accordance with a provision of the Sharia).

As human beings we are of course unhappy that our daughter took this step. But we take the Bible seriously when it says in all things to give thanks to God. So even in these difficult circumstances we thank God for his blessings and for our family. God has his own purposes for everything, and we can thank him even when we don't know the reasons, even when what happens is so painful. Even in the pain the peace of God reigns within us. In fact, when friends come to comfort us, we are often able to comfort them, and they leave being more encouraged than when they came.

One Moslem woman came to my wife in a triumphant mood over Jummai's conversion. But I think Gumi and his friends could be making a mistake in rejoicing too soon. God is sovereign, and he may have in mind for Jummai to learn the Koran, then come to genuine Christian faith and be more effective in reaching Moslems for Christ.

There have been concerns about why a publication funded and owned by the federal government of Nigeria should give such publicity to the story of a Christian girl's conversion to Islam. It was purely a provocation, aimed squarely not only at me but also at the Christians of Nigeria. All the publicity in Islamic publications shows how desperate they are about conversions.

This case is even bigger than what an ordinary conversion from Christianity would be. The conversion to Islam of Christopher Abashiya's daughter is so important to them because he was getting farther and farther out of their reach—but they could get back at him by bringing his daughter over to their side. Gumi was reported to have said that now that Jummai was a Moslem, he hoped I too would return to Islam. And in another journal Jummai was quoted as appealing to her parents to come back to Islam. Finally, Jummai paid a visit to our son Sam and tried to persuade him to convert to Islam.

The future of our country depends largely on whether Nigerians of different religions can live together in peace. Many Moslems make no secret of their intention to make the country wholly Islamic, and

Colonel Gaddafi of Libya said in Burundi that they must Islamize everybody on the African continent. If the Moslems would only recognize our country as a multi-religious society, it would be possible to live together with love and mutual respect, and there would be peace and stability in the country.

LATIN AMERICA

CHAPTER 11

THE CARROT
AND THE STICK
by Renaldo Perez

Introduction: In the three decades since the Cuban revolution, Castro's regime has evolved into what all Marxist-Leninist states have become: an economic failure with political power monopolized in the hands of a privileged oligarchy which disdains human rights.

As is common in Latin America the pre-Communist regime in Cuba was dominated by people who used their power to further their own interests rather than that of the country. This made persuasive the claims of the revolutionaries to be fighting for the interests of ordinary people. What the revolution actually did was substitute a new set of oppressors—one backed by both military aid and huge financial subsidies from the Soviet Union—for the old. Even today many Christians are taken in by the claim that in order

*to oppose the injustices of the Latin American
regimes it is necessary to support the Marxist-
Leninist opposition.*

*How are Christians able to conduct their
responsibilities to God in this environment of
great hostility? Renaldo Perez gives us some
insights into that question.*

• • •

*B*efore my conversion, I worked as an engineer for
the revolutionary Cuban government. In this capacity
I traveled to the USSR, Eastern Europe, and even Canada.
After I became a Christian I felt a special calling to
engage in the pastoral ministry. In my country all
Christians are disliked by the regime's leaders, but the
offense is much more serious when intellectuals or
professionals become believers. As an engineer, that
difference became very significant for me.

Immediately I came under constant surveillance. This
so hampered my effectiveness that I thought I could
serve our people better from outside the country.
Therefore I applied for permission to leave Cuba
permanently. The government granted this request
readily enough, and we made all the necessary
arrangements for our departure. Finally, we were at the
airport, ready to board the plane that would take my
family and me out of our homeland. As we walked
toward the airplane, government agents stopped us and
declared we would not be allowed to depart because of
security considerations. Our permission to leave was
revoked.

It shattered our expectations. But we took it as
confirmation that the Lord had work for us to do here. I
have been serving as a pastor in Cuba since then. Until
recently my family has lived in the basement of the
church I serve.

As a pastor I earn a wage of 150 pesos per month.

This is about average for Cuban workers. It allows us to rent a simple dwelling and buy the basic necessities of life. The state pays for our medical and educational expenses. But in the case of those who are not enthusiastic participants in the revolution—or who will not pretend to be such—these "rights" are manipulated so as to make it advisable to become more friendly to the state.

Money is not, by itself, enough to buy the necessities of life. Cubans also need a ration card issued by the state. This card allows us to purchase fixed quantities of about one hundred fifty items. Each person can buy some grain; one ounce of meat a week; one bar of Russian soap a month; three yards of material a year for babies' clothing and another three yards for diapers; one towel a year; one pair of shoes a year. Women can buy one brassiere per year, and men two sets of underwear or socks. One pastor I know has owned just one pair of pants and two shirts for seven years. Luxury items, such as stereos and refrigerators, can cost as much as one to two years' wages. People can qualify to purchase one of these appliances if they volunteer for government work brigades. Sometimes these articles can be had through the gifts of a relative or friend from abroad. When permission is granted, the purchase is made in local tourist stores for hard currency.

One of the hardships faced by Christians is their isolation from other believers on the outside. We receive radio programs from station HCJB in Ecuador, BONAIRE in Argentina, Family Radio in Oakland, California, and other radio ministries. These programs are very popular and help us overcome the effects of isolation. There is no way, of course, for us to receive Christian television.

As is typical of the constitutions of Communist countries, Cuba allows the freedom to "believe or not believe." But there are strict limitations on certain practices such as evangelism. The regime does not permit the preaching of the gospel either door to door or in public meetings. Believers might proclaim the faith to other individuals at school or work, but it is done at the risk of receiving demerits.

Preaching is allowed only within the four walls of the church building. Each service is attended by government informers who monitor the sermon to report items that might interest authorities. The state confines the public activities of the church to the worship service. It does not permit special events such as concerts or evangelistic campaigns. Sometimes exceptions are made when the authorities see the propaganda value in a particular event or when the security services can obtain information through surveillance.

Pastors with effective ministries are noticed by the state and given particular attention. Security officers are always on the lookout for ways to discredit them. They make use of "carrots" to entice pastors into cooperating with the regime, and "sticks" to frighten them into submission. These carrots are much more important than measures of open brutality. Our national leader, Fidel Castro, once put it this way: "We don't want martyrs; we want apostates."

The regime provides rewards for those who cooperate with it. Foreign travel, for example, is a highly prized benefit, but those who accept such rewards are viewed with suspicion by many believers. Apart from the propaganda value of having church leaders seen in foreign meetings, the state also benefits by using travelers as sources of information.

Our church is the property of the state as are all church buildings. These structures have been physically neglected for twenty-eight years, and many are seriously dilapidated.

Cuba does not have a legal Bible society. Nor are Bibles available for sale in bookstores. From time to time the government has permitted shipments of Bibles to be imported when it served their purposes. But only a very small percentage of our needs are met in this way. And a

church that is not part of the government-authorized
ecumenical council is likely to get nothing.

In order to solidify its hold on the country, the
government monopolizes all the organs of
communication. Political banners and posters are
everywhere. Radio and television are controlled by the
government and are full of political material. The
government makes use of various voluntary associations,
including religious and professional ones, and it is able
to establish communication channels through them.

Committees for the Defense of the Revolution (CDRs)
are found in every block or population center in Cuba.
Their purpose is to monitor all activity and (to the extent
possible) all the people in their area of responsibility.
The government claims that about 85 percent of the
population belongs to the CDRs. This high participation
rate comes from the progression of young people
through various organizations. Indoctrination begins in
the state nursery school and continues through
preschool, Young Pioneers, then the Union of Young
Communists. Finally, a small percentage become full
members of the Communist party.

Both students and workers have a file that follows
them throughout their lives. Being considered "religious"
is enough to earn a demerit either at school or work. No
Christian will be allowed to enter certain careers—
journalism or psychology, for example. For active
Christians the demerits are increased so that career and
educational opportunities become severely reduced. And
since pastors are required by law to report all changes in
membership each quarter, the government has an
updated list of people on whom "special education"
should be practiced. This can mean anything from
increased surveillance and ideological pressure from the
CDRs, to threats and even imprisonment.

The universities and training centers prepare
schoolteachers to give instruction in atheism and to
discourage and report anti-social behavior—including

evidences of Christian behavior. The children of Christian families are often singled out and ridiculed in front of their classmates, who are warned not to befriend them. The school administration uses the natural desire of students to have a sense of belonging by encouraging the joining of the Young Pioneers, the Communist youth movement. During the teen years when students begin experimenting with alcohol and immoral behavior, the Christian students stand out by refusing to do so. This provides further opportunity for ridicule and persecution by teachers and classmates.

When a Christian is imprisoned, the church sometimes fails to act as it should. Members may become timid and reserved in their dealings with the affected family in order not to be accused of a crime. Speaking with foreigners is most difficult because it can be used as evidence that this "anti-revolutionary" family is making contacts against the interests of the state.

Despite all these difficulties Christians can still have an influence on their society. When they do it is because they are faithful and because the Lord is faithful in empowering his people. Their family life is strong because of God's protection and strength. The church has grown under these conditions, in quality as well as in numbers. Believers tend to be very hot or very cold. Thank God, many in Cuba are hot.

CHAPTER 12

UNCERTAINTIES
UNDER CASTRO
by José Fuentes

Introduction: Totalitarian regimes are hard on Christians, but in many ways this simply reflects how hard they are on most of their citizens. In particular, the economic system flounders when economic life is placed under political control. Thus Christians, along with everyone else in the society, find much of their attention given to circumventing the roadblocks set up to prevent ordinary economic transactions.

Since the legal and administrative systems are made to serve the rulers rather than the requirements of justice, problems that in other countries would be relatively easy to solve are transformed into major difficulties. José Fuentes has chosen to highlight these economic and legal challenges of modern life in Cuba.

• • •

I welcome the chance to tell fellow believers in Christ what our life is like in Cuba. In some ways it is not easy here, but our lot is much better than in many places, and we are grateful to God for our blessings.

My wife, Elena, and I have four children: Eduardo is married to Carmen and they have a little daughter, not yet two years old. Our second son, Pablo, is in his second year of military duty. Teresa is in ninth grade, and our youngest, Delores, is in seventh.

We live on the second floor of a two-story house. The ground floor is old, dating from before the revolution. It is well built, nicely finished, and has very attractive decorating. Elena's mother lives there. The upper floor was built after the revolution by amateurs; it is solid but poorly finished. You can enter our quarters by a narrow concrete stairway on the outside of the house. The railing is made of left-over structural iron, and since the stairway is only about a foot wide, it was not put there for decorative reasons.

Our living room is a square, about seven feet on each side. We have three very small bedrooms. The bathroom is three feet by seven feet. It has a toilet (without a seat), a ceramic washstand (with only one faucet—cold), and a shower, also with only cold water. The kitchen is four feet by nine feet with a refrigerator, a simple wooden table and six chairs, and a two-burner stove which operates on kerosene. All the floors are cement.

Our furniture is old, nothing less than twenty years. All the upholstery has been renewed several times, usually by a family member or friend. The beds are only a box spring and mattress. We have no built-in closets. We keep our things on improvised shelves or a few old wooden wardrobes.

Paint is scarce in Cuba, and the exterior walls have not been painted in years. There are several colors on the inside which do not match; we use whatever paint appears on the market.

People who owned a house before the revolution

were allowed to keep it. But we can't sell the house privately; we can only exchange it with people who agree to the trade. A new house is almost impossible to find, so young couples who marry often live with one set of parents. Only after years of outstanding performance on the job will someone be allowed to enter a drawing for a house. The winner of the drawing receives the right (not the money) to buy the house.

The big economic problem of most Cubans is not so much money as the scarcity of things to buy. The ration book is as necessary for a shopping trip as the pocketbook. Extra ration coupons can be secured by those whose work performance is considered outstanding. There are also free markets where anyone with money can buy food and clothing, but the prices are several times as high as in the government markets and few people can afford much in them. Items such as furniture, refrigerators, cars, and electronic appliances can be bought only from official channels by merits that come from supervisors and officials. These merits are hard to obtain and usually require a long time, sometimes years, on the job and on extra duties in one's spare time. Most people don't bother to make the effort.

People with U.S. dollars or other hard currencies can buy almost anything they wish in special shops intended primarily for tourists and diplomats. Some Cubans deal in the black market for currency, buying dollars for up to ten times the official rate. With the dollars they can buy what they want at the special shops by using the services of tourists or embassy people with whom they cultivate relationships.

The amount of food provided by the ration book is barely enough for proper nutrition, and each item is available only on specific days. When the food arrives at the shop the amount is frequently less than is needed, so many people wait in line for hours before opening time. Someone who misses his turn may go for that month without that particular item, such as chicken or rice. To compensate, people buy extra amounts of food that is not rationed, such as bread or eggs. In spite of food shortages it is possible to find fat people in Cuba because the diet tends to be heavy on carbohydrates.

I work as a tractor operator in the construction industry. The hours are odd: I work from 4:30 A.M. to 8 P.M. These seem like terrible hours, but I work for one week and then take the next two weeks off.

The average Cuban income is not sufficient to live comfortably. But most find a way to make more money, even though private businesses are not permitted. In general Cubans earn part of their living by stealing from their employer, which is always the government. The practice is almost universal; even Christians allow themselves to get caught up in it. But stealing is just one of the many factors that reveal the state of our economic system.

Discrimination is common in hiring, firing, and promoting. Most workers are indifferent to their work performance since there are few incentives to do better. It is easy for Christians to excel because they tend to be better motivated, the motivation coming from within rather than on any economic reward. Many win prize competitions at work; yet, they are often prevented from receiving the prizes because of their faith. I have received a number of prizes at work and that has not made people happy. Two years ago I won a refrigerator, but the manager decided I had already won too much and instead cast lots for the appliance. To everyone's surprise I won the refrigerator anyway.

In the last few years a new boldness has developed among believers. Although the written laws and regulations do not discriminate between Christians and non-Christians, believers usually have low-paid jobs and are prevented from being promoted. Several times my boss and I have discussed this at length, and my persistence has made it easier for him to give in and obey the law than to continue to discriminate. The situation has become much better.

This evasion of legality in the economic sector has its counterpart in the legal sphere. When Christians are accused of breaking the law, the judicial system offers them a lawyer. But everyone understands that the lawyer serves the government prosecutor rather than the defendant. Some Christians therefore defend themselves rather than receiving the "help" of the lawyer offered by the government. The results have improved.

One example of this is a well-known evangelist in our area whose work has brought many people to faith in Christ. Four or five years ago he was holding an evangelistic and healing campaign which attracted three thousand people or more. Since the capacity of the church is only about three hundred, crowds gathered all around the building. After three days of successful meetings with many people coming to faith, the police came and arrested the evangelist. The campaign had to be canceled.

At his trial the prosecution charged the evangelist with three offenses: 1) Acting as a doctor without authorization from the health department; 2) leading a religious meeting outside of church buildings without written permission from the government; and 3) expressing to a public audience concepts that were ideologically contrary to the government. He decided not to use the government-provided lawyer but conducted his defense himself. We believe God gave him wisdom and boldness to speak with clarity. He refuted the charges, which were canceled. But the court gave him a five month sentence anyway for causing problems for government officials and wasting their time.

A similar event took place a few months ago. Municipal authorities gave an innocent evangelist a four month sentence. He appealed to a higher court and when he appeared for his hearing, a United Nations committee investigating human rights turned up after being alerted by friends of the accused man. Government officials at the trial saw the public relations difficulties, apologized to the evangelist, and dropped all charges. He then took advantage of the situation to request permission to attend a Christian convention and preach in the United States. Although he had been turned down for similar requests many times before, this time his request was granted.

When children reach secondary school age (twelve or thirteen) they are required to study away from their homes. They live in dormitories and do agricultural work to compensate for the cost of their studies. Sometimes this move can be postponed until the age of fifteen or sixteen. Those living in Havana may be allowed to remain in their homes because there are so many secondary schools in that region. But this exception seldom is granted to Christians.

As in most other things, the rules are flexible depending on the firmness of the local officials and the extent to which believers are willing to stand firm and run the risks required. We refused to allow our children to be sent away to the secondary school where sexual immorality is accepted and the general moral situation is bad. We told the authorities that we preferred to have their formal education stop than to have them exposed to an environment in which there was no concern for moral teachings or the Christian convictions of the family. As a result, our children are living at home and attending local schools.

All children are granted the "privilege" of wearing the red scarf which identifies them as *Pioneers*, members of the children's sector of the Communist party. Our children all refused to wear the red scarf and consequently were not permitted to attend the children's and youth camps. The church facilities they attend are not as good, but are much more wholesome.

The ability of Christians to obtain advanced training varies from province to province. Some in Havana have become university graduates. In other places this is impossible. I know several believers who have been expelled from universities for personal witnessing.

There are no restrictions on teaching religion in the home or church as long as nothing is directed against the government. There are a few exceptions: Jehovah's Witnesses, for example, are banned. Also the church may not offer such activities as Sunday schools for children unless their parents are involved in the church, and it is not permitted to go out and invite the public to attend. People can legally teach their children about the faith, but there will likely be consequences if they do so. Employers and officials threaten Christians with the loss of their jobs or of educational rights. These threats are increasingly being overcome by appeals to higher levels. The trouble is that too many people allow the pressures to demoralize and silence them.

Our church is a mission effort of a Methodist church. Three years ago we had twenty-five members, a number which had remained fairly constant for twenty years. We now have about seventy members. Part of the reason for our growth is that we have had access to books from the outside that have helped us understand better how the Christian life is to be lived. Of course, these books cannot be imported through official channels.

Our church building is about twenty-five feet wide by seventy feet in length. It is simple but well built, with a cement tile floor and wooden windows. The roof is concrete. The wooden pews are as old as the church, dating from before the revolution. The pulpit, altar, and platform decorations have seen better days, but are carefully looked after, since religious decorations are no longer available. As far as I know there has not been a single church constructed since the Castro regime took over. It's very difficult, sometimes impossible, to get authorization for remodeling or expansion of church facilities.

A church in Oriente obtained permission from the Ministry of Construction to expand its building after years of refusal. When they had knocked down the walls and built new columns and a roof, the Ministry canceled the building license and stopped construction. Numerous appeals over the last three years have gone unheeded. But the Lord has used the situation in an interesting way. Since the building has no walls the preaching and hymns are heard in the neighborhood much more clearly than if the church had been enclosed. More people are hearing the gospel this way.

All our churches existed before the revolution and are registered with the government. To the best of my knowledge there are no underground churches. The government has files on all the churches, but I doubt that many are complete or up-to-date. Some denominations have joined the Ecumenical Council of Cuba which stresses the importance of maintaining good relations with the government. Others believe that this necessarily compromises their beliefs and will not join. Our denomination belongs to the council.

Religious meetings are not permitted outside of church buildings. Occasionally small groups of five to ten people meet in a home. But this is only for informal fellowship, never for a worship service. Even at that, these meetings are frequently canceled because of government pressure. Anyone who persists in spite of the pressure can expect to be taken to the police station for interrogation, exhortation, or threats.

One of our most urgent needs is for Bibles and Christian literature. Our family has become a distributor for materials that have reached as far as the eastern end of Cuba. The people who receive these materials are very grateful and appreciative. They cover them with plastic, then pass them around from family to family. We keep detailed records of who has what material, so that on any given day we know where everything is. Two pastors have acquired copying machines and are now reproducing much of this material.

The government requires that pastors be licensed

before they can exercise their offices. Anyone preaching without a license can be imprisoned. It is actually not hard to obtain a license, and most pastors prefer to have one, even though many do not like the implication that the state has a right to license ministers of the gospel.

Special permission is required if we want to have meetings that bring together church people from different cities. Sometimes this is granted and sometimes not. It is one of many uncertainties in our lives.

We have not had the troubles that some countries have in worshiping freely; we go to church without interference. As far as I know, pastors have never been imposed on a congregation by the government. Still, the restrictions on theological education have made it necessary to ordain ministers who are not as qualified as they should be.

We have been able to support fellow believers who get in trouble with the authorities. If they are under arrest we take them food and water. We have a network that tries to keep informed about trials. And there are ways of producing social pressures on judges that moderate the kind of harsh and unfair judgments that they might otherwise issue. Sometimes people who speak out against injustice are thrown into prison for long periods of time and without a fair trial. At times, this becomes known to the world. But many are known only to a small number of Cuban believers.

Because of his Christian convictions, Pablo has come under some pressure in his military service. In the military, as in the rest of Cuba, corruption is rampant. But he has resisted the temptations to join in the corruption and, along with three other Christian soldiers, has remained firm in honest behavior and hard work. As a result he is very well treated and even given extra privileges, such as living in his own home.

The experience of Pablo as well as that of others has convinced me that when Christians are bold and responsible they do not always receive bad treatment.

Their boldness is closely related to the closeness of their walk with God. Other believers are not as courageous and end up in difficult circumstances. One result is that despite their convictions they end up on such government projects as International Missions, which place them in Nicaragua, Angola, or similar places where the Castro regime is advancing its interests.

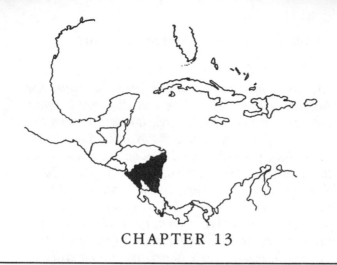

CHAPTER 13

REPRESSION WITH
A "HUMAN FACE"
by John Bent

Introduction: Hope blossomed in Nicaragua when, in July 1979, the Sandinista revolution overthrew the corrupt and brutal Somoza regime. Although some Sandinista leaders were committed Marxist-Leninists, other groups were represented as well, including Christians. Indeed, four Catholic priests occupied government posts. Many people in neighboring countries, as well as in other parts of the world, thought this diversity of views among the leadership would prevent the kind of repression standard in other Communist regimes. Church groups in Europe and North America have led the way in giving the benefit of the doubt to the Sandinistas, contributing considerable political support as well as material goods to try to bail out the shattered Nicaraguan economy.

Much of this support stems from the influence of liberation theology. While this theology is often associated with Latin America, it originated in the thinking of European and North American intellectuals who then influenced students from Latin America.[1] There are differences of emphasis within liberation theology, but all call for helping the poor and stress the biblical denunciations of oppression. This strikes a responsive chord among Latin Americans who suffer under tyrannies. But liberation theology also hearkens uncritically to Marxism's promise of liberation, and even turns a blind eye toward the oppression of such regimes as Fidel Castro's Cuba.

Contrary to the reports of political pilgrims from the north who visit Nicaragua and see what the Sandinistas want them to see, there has been considerable repression in the country, causing many moderates to desert the movement (and thereby intensifying the repression). Help from the Soviet bloc has gone largely to building the mightiest military force in the region.

This is being written only weeks after the defeat of the Sandinistas in the election of 1990. But while there is much to be thankful for in the passing of a Marxist-Leninist regime, the Sandinistas have pledged themselves to continue their opposition. Continued frustration at the ballot box could again prompt them to turn to the gun.

John Bent's experiences show how the combination of repression with some freedom of action—perhaps we could call it repression with a human face—works out in practice.

Mr. Bent has worked for a copper mine, constructed a church, taught mathematics, and served at different times as school principal and a musician. He is a folklorist and ethno-

musicologist. He has done research on the biological aspects of music and is writing a book on how different types of music affect people. The Moravian Church, to which he belongs, has been in Nicaragua since 1849, when Moravians arrived from Germany. The church is concentrated on the Caribbean side of the country.

• • •

I am from Bluefields in eastern Nicaragua on the Caribbean coast. About twenty-five thousand people live here, 80 percent of whom are black. English is the major language, reflecting the area's British settlement.

Shortly before the revolution succeeded, Sandinistas began introducing cocaine and marijuana into the east coast. I believe they did this in order to reduce the people's analytical abilities and make them easier to manipulate. To combat this problem, some of our people in early 1978 founded the Southern Indigenous Creole Community of Nicaragua. I began working with this organization, teaching people that using drugs was a way of submitting to domination. Since these drugs were sold mainly to blacks, we considered the drug trade a form of racism.

Part of the problem was that blacks needed to know their own history in order to develop some pride in who they were. Several of us, including a Roman Catholic priest and a Moravian bishop, founded the History of Culture Institute of the Atlantic Coast of Nicaragua. Our weekly meetings lasted four or five hours each and were held in different communities. We tried to give black youth their identity. The Moravians had taught them about God but not about who they were. We also taught them a Christian perspective without trying to steer them to one denomination or another. All this activity did not go unnoticed. As the war approached its final stage, the police questioned us as suspected Sandinistas.

On July 19, 1979, the Sandinistas took over. The civil war had devastated the country and in our area at least, the economy was paralyzed. Serious food shortages arose. The Southern Indigenous Creole Community organized a sealift to bring supplies from Colombia; the Colombian Red Cross gave us food. The Sandinistas viewed me as cooperative during this period.

During the last stages of the civil war the university at Bluefields was closed so I began teaching at the Moravian high school. The Sandinistas approached me and proposed that I become part of the plan to establish a model society for Central America. A former friend of mine who had joined the Sandinistas explained that to do this I would have to give up Christian principles and instead adopt socialist ones. They were ready to supply all the books and instructional materials I needed. I told them I could not agree to give up my Christian convictions.

My refusal to work with the Sandinistas was enough to mark me as an enemy, but a further complication arose. In their recruiting effort, they had described to me their plans for indoctrinating the area with Marxist teaching. That made it important to send me away. So they transferred me from Bluefields to Managua to work on the literacy campaign, a legal move because the Ministry of Education subsidized the Moravian school where I was working. When I objected to the ideology of the literacy campaign I was transferred to the Ministry of Culture—the division of black culture and research. As part of my duties, the Ministry sent me to the Pearl Lagoon region to conduct a census.

When I passed through Bluefields on my way back to Managua from the Pearl Lagoon, I found a demonstration in progress. Tensions had been mounting over the numbers of Cubans who had moved in. They had provoked a series of incidents, and many jobs were taken away from our people and given to them. A big demonstration and a general strike were planned for the area just as I came through town, in September 1980.

Several of us organized a meeting—a sort of people's assembly—in order to reestablish order with justice. We invited government officials to make sure they understood the problem. After the officials had heard us they promised to get rid of the Cubans. In order to make sure the government followed through on this I telephoned the Minister of the Interior in Managua and spoke to an officer who assured me they would take care of the problem. A few hours later three hundred soldiers flew into Bluefields and got off the planes shooting. They arrested a number of people, including the board of the Southern Indigenous Creole Community—which included me. They came to my house and said the commander wanted to talk to me. One of the officers described me as dangerous. So they handcuffed me and flew me to Managua with the others.

Torture was one of the jail officials' standard techniques. Many people were beaten. An Anglican priest in the next cell was repeatedly threatened with shooting if he continued to pray. The type of torture depended on who the person was and how much support he had on the outside. Since they intended to use me for propaganda purposes they could leave no telltale marks.

Instead they kept me from sleeping. When I started to drop off the guards shouted at me, banged on the doors, picked me up, and walked me up and down the jail. After I wore out they questioned me and made all sorts of wild accusations. They said they had proof of my crimes but they needed confirmation and also other names. They tried to discredit the rest of the community leadership in order to break our sense of solidarity.

One interrogator told me I had been brainwashed in order to brainwash others. That made me dangerous. They criticized what they called the "North American Bible" which they said was written and distributed for brainwashing purposes. I was not permitted to ask questions. They asked me about the location of the arms I would use to take over Bluefields, about who gave me the arms, the identity of the CIA agent I was connected with, who were my connections in the rest of the country, where they could find the three hundred men who were supposed to be going into battle against the Sandinistas on the east coast. They asked me these things over and over again. There was little dialogue; I was simply ordered to answer the questions.

On one occasion the Sandinista official Tomas Borge came to visit. He asked similar questions and then stood for half an hour giving me a speech about his knowledge of the situation. He asked me if I didn't know that gringos were killing my people and why was I pro-gringo, why was I an anti-Communist. Every time I tried to answer he cut me off. He was the only one allowed to speak.

One day he invited me to have lunch with him. I was taken from jail and escorted to him. He asked if I would go back to Bluefields with him and tell the people that the Sandinista government was good, that although we had misunderstood each other, they were willing to talk with us and work with us for the benefit of the community. I said no. We had lost confidence in the Sandinistas and did not know what to expect from them. The policies they had announced conflicted with much of what they were doing. How could I endorse them? That was the extent of our meeting.

The Sandinistas established a special "people's court" to take care of political cases like mine. They condemned me without a trial. (The court was abolished in March 1988 but those it had condemned were not freed.) Three charges were brought against me: violating the state security law; breaking the international security law; and violating the conspiracy law. I was found guilty on all three counts with a combined sentence of nine years, which my lawyer afterwards got reduced to three. (You are allowed a lawyer *after* sentencing, not before.) I was also accused of having arms and a private army, but no evidence for this was offered and I was not convicted on that charge.

Some time after this a businessman was murdered, and I was implicated in the investigation. The authorities returned me to the first jail and questioned me there for two days, ten hours a day. A number of us were placed in isolation, one to a cell. This special section of the jail was underground, well guarded with German Shepherds and Dobermans.

The isolation system did not work as well as the jailers intended. Prisoners had ways of communicating through the toilets. In each cell a hole in the ground contained a box with a trap. These led to a main pipe which connected thirty cells on the same line. A prisoner would wash out the trap in his cell and then put his head into it. You would say, "Number twenty-eight" and then give your name. Everyone knew who was there. We memorized the names—we had no paper, pencil, or books, and it was dark in the cells. Even so, it was difficult to sleep under those conditions. We lost sense of time. After seventeen days I was sent back to the large jail.

That facility housed six men to each one-man cell. Two stood while four slept. There was little food. The Red Cross provided rice and beans but this soon ran out. Families of prisoners brought food when allowed, fifteen days worth at a time. They might not be allowed back for thirty days.

When foreigners and international groups visited, a cow would be killed and we would eat well. The arrival of journalists prompted even better treatment. Then we were given opportunities to exercise, even to play baseball. Our jailers stressed reeducation. In fact, the jails were called Centers of Rehabilitation and Reeducation.

Anyone who raised his head over the bars after 10 P.M. could expect shots to be fired his way. Some people were taken out in the middle of the night and disappeared. We never found out what happened to them, but we know that the followers of the former dictator, Somoza, were killed.

After a month I was transferred to a bigger jail which held about four thousand inmates, mostly political prisoners. There I found thirty Christians worshiping God together every morning. We formed a choir and made plans to evangelize the jail.

The thirty Christians started a Bible school and then began multiplying. After two months authorities confiscated all our Bibles and religious books. By then there were three hundred of us. The confiscations produced more solidarity among the prisoners and that made them more open to the gospel. Believers multiplied all the more. When I left after eleven months, seven hundred of the four thousand prisoners identified themselves as evangelicals. In addition there were two or three hundred Catholics. Both groups were very evangelistic.

In order to break up the Christian impact, the authorities sent us to other jails. This proved to be a mistake because it spread the evangelistic effort. They ended up with thousands of Christians to contend with. The head of the jail gave us permission to baptize converts, but he lost his job for doing so.

My release came in September 1981 when the Minister of the Interior visited me in jail and said I would be removed because I was a trouble maker. They thought they could watch me better on the outside.

For a time after my release I participated in an opposition party, but I soon left because of its disunity. I began to study theology and worked for a Christian center for the rehabilitation of drug addicts and prostitutes. I joined a group called the National Council of Evangelical Pastors of Nicaragua (CNPEN). We worked hard to study our situation theologically in order to seek an alternative to liberation theology. Our only alternatives before could not meet the needs of our society.

Liberation theology was taking over among intellectuals, especially in Latin American seminaries. We are still working on our theology, but we are convinced the answer lies in a world view formed by the biblical message as expressed in the reformed faith. Liberation theology fails because it finds its hope in man and not God.

The Sandinista regime tried a variety of methods to deal with the church. The regime was under such close scrutiny from the outside and was so dependent upon public relations for its foreign support that it tried to control the churches with as little overt oppression as possible. The harshest measures were used when there appeared to be a reasonable chance of keeping them out of sight.

More effective has been the effort to work with churches and church-related groups willing to be compromised. Liberation theology has effectively convinced a number of Christians that it is possible to reconcile Marxism with Christianity. An organization called the Evangelical Committee for Aid and Development (CEPAD) has been especially useful to them. Although it claims about two hundred members, it has the ear of numerous religious groups in North America and Europe. A great deal of church money is funneled through CEPAD, and much of it is used for Sandinista purposes. The group features a great diversity of people and many are sincere Christians. Its guiding philosophy, however, seems to be that in order to survive you must make your peace with a regime that otherwise would be glad to see the church disappear. One CEPAD official told the head of the Sandinistas that CNPEN was controlled by the CIA.

Our teaching now centers on understanding the world and our society through a biblical world view. There is much interest in this in CNPEN. We are trying to provide a Christian alternative to both the Sandinistas and the Contras. We summarize this perspective as "Discipling the Nation for Christ." We believe that is what is meant by the great commission. This approach is proving quite fruitful.

Notes

1. On this point, which is not widely known, see Edward Norman, *Christian Faith and the World Order* (Oxford: Oxford University Press, 1979), pp. 46-70.

EASTERN EUROPE

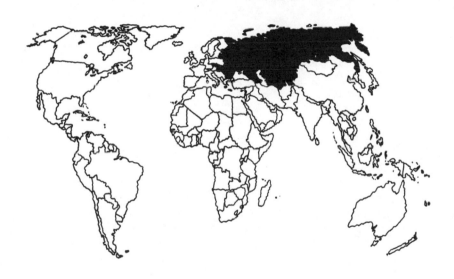

CHAPTER 14

A TRAFFIC ACCIDENT, ROMANIAN STYLE

by Peter Dugulescu

Introduction: A one-party Communist state since 1947, Romania was governed for almost twenty-five years by Nicolai Ceaucescu. Persecution of the church was less severe at the time of his execution in December 1989 than earlier, but Romania was still the most resolutely Stalinist of the Warsaw Pact nations in its approach to religious bodies. The Romanian Orthodox Church is dominant in the country although a number of Protestant churches also exist.

Although the official Romanian Orthodox Church is sadly deficient in spiritual life and is dominated by the state, a branch of it is very different in nature. Called the Lord's Army, it dates from a revival that broke out in Orthodoxy in the 1920s and is characterized by evangelical fervor, a strong devotion to the Bible, and a spirit of independence from the authorities. Even before the Communist regime took over, the group met fierce opposition from the Orthodox hierarchy and was outlawed by the government. Nevertheless, it is believed to be still growing; some estimate its size to be 300,000 people out of a total population of some 19 million.

More than most countries, Romania is a bundle of contradictions. With the exception of Hungary its neighbors are all Slavic, while its language and culture are Latin. It is the eastern-most outpost of Latin culture. For many years the Romanian government refused to participate in Warsaw Pact maneuvers, and it did not allow Soviet troops on its territory. It has also conducted other foreign policy initiatives at variance with its allies. This show of independence was part of a carefully conducted campaign to bring foreign policy benefits and hard currency into Romania. The policy succeeded in gaining favorable trade status with the United States, which helped its economic position (but which in most other respects has been a disaster). This status was terminated in 1988 when Romania's anti-religious campaigns finally proved too odious for the U.S. Congress to stomach.

With most of the east European Communist economies appearing increasingly decrepit, Romania occupies a category of its own. Food shortages are present everywhere, and consumer goods are almost non-existent. Fuel shortages mean that houses and public buildings go unheated. People die of exposure in hospitals because of the cold, and the infant mortality rate has soared. The general suffering is intense. Christian agencies from the west which formerly delivered Bibles in unofficial shipments now concentrate on food shipments.

Communist regimes for the most part learned that silent pressures against Christians can be more effective than mass killings. They cause far less difficulty with foreign governments and organizations, and can usually be hidden from sight. But these regimes still bore an iron fist beneath the velvet glove. Beatings and jailings continued to take place, especially in the provinces far from the capital cities where foreign journalists live. And occasionally the regime found it expedient to resort to murder. Peter Dugulescu tells us how his evangelistic activities prompted the Romanian government to order his execution in a staged road accident.

The current scene in Romania, six months after the revolution, is uncertain. After the national elections, former officials of the Ceaucescu regime still rule in Bucharest. And the bureaucracy controlling the churches, far from being dismantled, has been upgraded to ministry status. The mood among many Christians is somber as they see little evidence from the new regime that it intends to respect their rights and obligations.

● ● ●

I pastor the First Baptist Church in Timisoara, the fourth largest city in Romania. It lies in the southwest part of the country, near Yugoslavia, about 350 miles from Bucharest. As a university center it is an important city even apart from its size. I am forty-three years of age. My wife Maria, and I have three children: Ligia is eighteen, Cristina sixteen, and Cristinel fourteen.

I was converted to faith in Christ at the age of twenty-one in the same church that I now serve as pastor. Afterwards I went to seminary in Bucharest. Two years ago I began to serve this church, having been called from another.

Our situation in Romania can be very difficult. Active pastors with growing ministries, especially those who attract young people, have many pressures put on them. And if their activities extend outside their church into other areas, the authorities can be quite forceful in expressing their displeasure.

One of the things authorities hate the most is evangelistic activity; it conflicts with the Communist party conviction that religion comes from the superstitious past and will be rejected by an increasingly educated population. Our Baptist churches frequently hold evangelistic campaigns. A church designates a particular week for evangelism, and each night an evangelist from another town preaches the gospel. Of course, it is impossible to advertise this, or even to put up signs, but the people of the church bring friends or acquaintances to hear the preaching. It is one of the most important means we have to spread the gospel. The authorities have not been successful in finding a way to stop us from having these services, although they hinder us by banning signs and posters. They have devoted a lot of effort to intimidating the evangelists, usually by threats, but also by stronger measures.

Therefore, it was not surprising when a policeman told me that if I did not stop my evangelistic activities I would have a car accident. I could either pay heed to what he told me, or a truck or bus would hit my car and that would be the end of me. This seemed to be a case of obeying either God or man, so I did not think I could in good conscience do what they asked of me.

One afternoon in September 1985, several months after my conversation with the policeman, I left another church where I had filled in as preacher. My wife and son were with me in the car. Upon leaving the church we turned onto a one-way street. As I drove slowly down the street I noticed a bus coming around the corner to my left. I stopped but the bus did not. The driver could have hit the back of the car, but instead turned the wheel and hit the front door on the driver's side. We heard a tremendous noise, the door caved in, and the impact broke my arm in two places. Then we choked on fumes. The left side of the car was destroyed.

In spite of the terrible way the driver drove the bus, at first I thought this was an ordinary accident. I did not connect it to the threat I had received. But in talking over the incident with a Christian friend several days later, we saw that it could not have been an accident.

In the first place, the bus had no business being where it was. It carried no passengers. The driver said he was on his way to the garage, but the garage was in another direction. And if the driver had kept to the rules of the road he would not have driven through the intersection. Immediately after the accident a police car came on the scene—*before* anyone called the police station. The police did not follow their normal procedures in accidents. They did not measure the distances or perform other normal tests. One policeman said it was too bad that the bus driver did not stop, but I saw him stop, so that was not the problem. The policeman said he would be around to see me in the hospital the next day.

The next day arrived, and the policeman did not come—another departure from the rules. Neither did the bus driver visit me. Normally, the bus driver would turn up to give evidence to the police. Finally, after my first operation, the police chief came to my hospital room and asked to see my driver's license. He said the accident was not my fault, but he didn't return the license to me. "What kind of a man is this bus driver?" I asked the police chief. "He crashed his bus into my car, broke my arm, and didn't even come to see me in the hospital." A few hours later the bus driver arrived. But he came for me to sign a paper. He wanted us to sign a statement saying that both of us were guilty of causing the accident. I realized what they were trying to do, and I refused to sign. If I acknowledged that I was partly to blame for the accident I would have no grounds to complain later that the bus driver had crashed into me deliberately.

Afterwards I asked a close friend to visit the bus driver and talk to him about the crash. My friend looked the driver right in the eye and asked him, "Was it just an accident you caused or was it something more?" The man became frightened, and my friend knew then that our suspicions were correct.

Later the bus driver came to visit me again at the hospital. Some relatives and church members were with me at the time. In the presence of everyone I said to him: "I know you tried to take my life. But I don't hate you. I am a Christian, and I love you. I won't hurt you." Then I asked him questions about his wife and children. He didn't deny that he had tried to kill me. I told him that those who paid him are well off financially in the kind of work they do, whereas the crash had cost me much in medical costs and in suffering. And in six months there would be another operation. I told him that God would supply all my needs, but that he was lost without Christ and without hope.

My next problem was getting back my driver's license. They told me they sent it to another city. A friend drove me to the police station in that city, and again we asked for the license. But they said I could only have a license if a took an examination, just like a beginner. They also required me to produce my medical records.

I refused to accept these conditions and told them that if they did not hand over the license I would write letters of protest to the president of the country and to the minister of interior affairs. This statement didn't move them. My lawyer wrote those letters for me, in which we accused the police of attempted murder and asked for a full investigation of the incident. According to administrative rules, the government is required to answer petitions like this within sixty days. Three years later, I still have yet to heard a word. But two weeks after leaving the police station I was called and asked to retrieve my driver's license.

My hand was in such terrible shape after the crash that I went back in for a second operation six months later. In a complicated procedure they took bone from my right thigh and used it to repair the arm. During the operation the oxygen tank ran empty. The anesthetist said there was no more oxygen in the hospital.

A Christian nurse present during the operation told me two days later what had happened. She screamed when she saw that the oxygen had run out and that I was starting to die. She quickly ran to grab another tank, brought it into the operating room, and they hooked it up.

Later I spoke to other doctors, and they confirmed my suspicions about this second operation. Since the accident had failed they were trying to do the job again in the hospital. My arm is still not straight and is very weak. The doctors offered to do an operation to make it right, but I said no thanks. On a trip to Germany I was able to have power steering put in the car so it wouldn't be so difficult to drive with my bad arm. Christians in England paid for the work.

These efforts at intimidation have completely failed. The government took our old church building for a redevelopment project but allowed us to buy a house. We have since expanded the house for our church and soon will be dedicating it. It is one of the largest churches in Romania, with more than one thousand seats.

As word of this and other attempted killings spreads in the West, it becomes increasingly clear that Romania's claims of religious liberty are patently false. That makes it more difficult for the government to try the same thing again, although violence still occurs when the authorities think they can get away with it. I still travel to other towns for evangelistic meetings and so do my colleagues. The Lord's work goes on in Romania despite government attempts to stop it. That shows where the real sovereignty lies.

CHAPTER 15

VANYA MEETS THE KGB

by Irina Andreevna Pogodina

Introduction: The Russian revolution is now three-quarters of a century old. The Soviet regime was erected on the ruins of a short-lived social democratic government that had replaced the centuries-old tsarist monarchy. It came in with both fervent opposition and enthusiastic support from the outside. One group saw the revolution as the triumph of barbarism and the end of Christian civilization in Russia. The other believed it would bring in a new age of peace and justice along with a kind of equality that had never been known. Much of the writing that hailed the formation of the Soviet state spoke of the "new man" that Soviet society would create and thereby perfect itself. The bitter experience of the decades have shown this latter position to be a delusion.

To understand Soviet brutality to the church

we must first understand its brutality toward the whole society. In the 1930s Stalin's policies killed millions of Soviet citizens through starvation, mistreatment in the labor camps and prisons, and shooting. Hardly a family remained untouched. Whole villages were wiped out. The number of the dead by the time of Stalin's demise in 1953 exceeded twenty million—more than the country lost in World War II.

The current situation under President Gorbachev is much better than it has been in many years. This thaw should be received with gratitude but not with blinders. There have been several other thaws in Soviet history. The early years of the revolution were times of revival for evangelical Protestants as the regime concentrated on destroying the Russian Orthodox Church. But then the Protestants' turn came. All segments of Christianity had virtually ceased open worship by the time of World War II.

But the German attack caught the regime so unprepared—many thousands of Soviet citizens welcomed the invading armies as liberators and some German army units were made up entirely of Russians—that Stalin made significant concessions to the church in order to gain support for the war effort. Consequently by 1945 there was a healthy church movement; some historians speak of a "revival" during this period. After the war Stalin cracked down hard once again, especially on some segments of the church. The Ukrainian Catholic Church and the Ukrainian Orthodox Church, for example, were outlawed completely, and the remnants merged with the Russian Orthodox Church.

People in the West ordinarily think of Khrushchev's period in the fifties and sixties as a time of liberalization after Stalinism. But

Khrushchev launched a renewed and sustained persecution against the church; about half the Orthodox churches in the country were closed down between 1959 and 1964, and most of them remain so.

In the current thaw there have been numerous positive developments. The number of Christians in the labor camps and psychiatric "hospitals" is down considerably compared with just a short time ago; some observers believe they are all free. Yet believers in the Soviet Union are far more cautious than many church people in the West. They don't know if Gorbachev will last and they're not sure that these policies will remain if he does.

One of the most serious problems facing Christians in closed countries is the lack of Bibles and other literature, even though such material is now openly imported and even printed in the Soviet Union. Increasingly, in the expectation of a much-liberalized new law on religious associations—promised for several years but not yet here—people ignore the law, and the authorities seem not to be inclined to enforce it.

Nobody knows how long these much-improved conditions will endure. Even now the news is not entirely good; beatings and even killings by KGB squads have persisted at least as recently as late 1989, a fact not widely known in the West.

Irina Pogodina's story gives us a good look at the activities of a family that has been actively engaged in Bible distribution before the current thaw.

• • •

*M*y husband, Ivan (everyone calls him Vanya), is a tall, solidly built man, an imposing figure with his brown, now slightly greying beard, his pronounced Slavic cheekbones, and his sparkling bright blue-grey eyes. In medieval Russia it was considered an insult to God for a man to shave his beard, and although things have changed a lot since then, all priests and deacons in the Russian Orthodox Church as well as a large number of male believers grow beards.

Vanya was born during the Great Patriotic War (World War II) into a comparatively prosperous family which owned a large apartment in an elegant old house just off Moscow's Tsvetnoy Boulevard. They were not believers. On the other hand, I was born into a Christian family and was a believer from an early age. This caused much difficulty in the early years of our marriage.

Vanya's early training was as a musician. He showed great promise, but a freak accident ruined his career just as he was about to join a major orchestra, the Leningrad Philharmonic. He was helping my brother build a dacha when he fell off the roof, breaking both a leg and an arm. His injuries never healed properly.

Shortly before the birth of our third child, Tanya, in 1973, I managed to persuade Vanya to go with me to the nearby Yelokhovskii Cathedral for the Easter service. This began late Saturday night. The building was packed to overflowing, and I was afraid we would not be able to get past the crowds and into the building to hear the Patriarch himself lead worship. Outside, it was dark, damp, and cold; inside all was ablaze with light, the light of countless candles and the shining reflections of the gilt of the icons. Amidst the glorious harmony of the choir and the fragrant smell of incense and candle wax, the words boomed forth, "Khristos voskrese!"—Christ is risen—to be echoed from the congregation, "Vistine voskrese!"—He is risen indeed.

Having stood up for a long time I was becoming very tired and desired to go back home. Vanya, however, wanted to stay. Just from glancing at his face, I knew that he had somehow changed from within. My prayers had been answered—the darkness was past, light had come.

Christ was risen indeed—and for Vanya.

For Vanya, the following months were the happiest in his life. The birth of Tanya filled him with wonder and awe at the miracle of new life. This seemed all the more tremendous because of the new life he could feel welling up inside him. What a fool he'd been to consider everything empty and futile just because he could no longer play the cello. If only he had turned to Christ before. Vanya started going to church several times a week and was soon accepted into the Cathedral Choir.

In 1974, with two other Christian musicians, Volodya and Pasha, Vanya began collecting old church choral music with the intention of having it published and performed. The following year, he wrote an article on the subject of medieval Russian church music, which was later translated into English and German. Over the next four years or so, the three friends traveled to many remote places collecting pieces of old music.

These trips not only opened Vanya's eyes to the beauty and richness of Russia's religious past, but to the tragedy of her religious present. At home in Moscow, my mother Natalya Fyodorovna's Bible always lay open before the icons and Vanya had his own New Testament. Yet on these summertime trips, he met countless Christians who not only didn't have their own Bibles and prayer books, but who hadn't read the Holy Scriptures since childhood. True, small numbers of Bibles were sometimes printed or even imported amidst much publicity, but most of these ended up in seminary libraries or in storage. Some printed in the USSR were actually exported to give the impression the country had a surplus; yet on many occasions Vanya saw whole New Testaments copied out by hand!

Vanya soon began to feel great sorrow for his fellow Christians and resolved to do everything he could to help those in need and to rear his children in the Orthodox faith. It was then that he understood what had caused me so much anxiety over the years; not only was no provision made for the religious upbringing of the children, but it was illegal for parents to "indoctrinate their sons and daughters with Christian myths."

Vanya once persuaded his brother Kostya to go with him to the church of St. Nicholas to hear the inspired teaching of Fr. Dmitri Dudko. Fr. Dudko realized that young people didn't go to church because they found the service strange, old-fashioned, and irrelevant. Therefore he began some remarkably popular question-and-answer sessions after evening service. He was finally removed by the authorities and sent to a country parish outside Moscow. Vanya was greatly influenced by these discourses and the need to make Christianity relevant for the young people.

Around 1980, largely as a response to Dudko's influence, Vanya began writing short stories and articles about the Christian faith for Soviet young people and children. Several of his friends read these short pieces and arranged to help him get them printed. This had to be done in the utmost secrecy, as the state maintains strict control over all means of publication. For example, it is illegal to use a photocopier (if one can be found!) without official permission. The only way that such things as Vanya's short stories could be printed in the USSR was as *samizdat*—illegally on typewriters and underground printing presses. Over the next few years, Vanya managed to write six more stories and a short novel called *The Large Forest*.

At about that time the KGB began a major "clean-up" of many prominent Orthodox Christians, the most well-known of whom were Father Dudko, Alexander Ogorodnikov, Lev Regelson and Father Gleb Yakunin. Among the many others to be arrested were Vanya's two colleagues Pasha Morgunov and Volodya Shapochkin, both of whom were arrested for "producing and distributing slanderous anti-Soviet propaganda." Pasha was imprisoned for a couple of years and then was allowed to emigrate. Volodya was put in a psychiatric hospital near Minsk. Nobody knows what has become of him or where he is.

On several occasions, Vanya had seen a black Volga parked just outside our house, each time with the same two men inside. But he thought nothing of it. Once his editor called him to the office and told him to watch his ways or he could lose his job. Then for a few days, Vanya was followed almost everywhere he went. The only way he could get rid of them was by going into a store and joining one of the long queues. Nine times out of ten, the men in the car got bored and disappeared. Vanya really thought he would be arrested next. Had Volodya or Pasha cracked under pressure and told everything? Suddenly, everything stopped and life returned to normal. It must have been a warning shot by the KGB.

One day in May 1983, Vanya returned home to find two smartly dressed men sitting in the kitchen talking to me. They rose from the table and introduced themselves as fellow Orthodox Christians from Paris. Vanya smiled uneasily and sat down. From what they said it seemed a copy of the stories and *The Large Forest* itself had been smuggled out and were being translated. A friend, whom they could not name, had told them where the Pogodins lived. The two men, a tall bald one who was called Henri and a younger one with a moustache who called himself by the very un-French name of Vitali, explained that they had specially come to Moscow to ask if they could help their Russian brothers and sisters by publishing the works in the west and then secretly bringing them into the Soviet Union. Vanya's heart missed a beat. Vitali added that the operation would involve meticulous planning and the utmost caution.

If they really were Frenchmen who had traveled the length of Europe to ask if they could help the Russian Church, then all our prayers had been answered. But if this was just a KGB ploy, then Vanya's head was as good as on the block. What should he do? I went to the stove in the corner of the tiny kitchen and lifted from it a bubbling pot of steaming borscht and placed it on the table next to a loaf of brown bread and some sausage. Without prompting, the two men rose with Vanya and all crossing themselves before the icon of the Savior began to recite the set prayer for meal times. For the first time since childhood, Vanya kept his eyes open. The two men certainly seemed sincere Christians, but how was it they spoke without a trace of an accent? All bowed, crossed themselves again, and sat down.

"Where did you learn to speak such good Russian?" I asked.

"From our parents," replied Henri, "they were Russian émigrés."

"Henri here spoke Russian before he knew any French," added Vitali with a grin.

Vanya's anxiety vanished. They were genuine.

After the meal, they began discussing plans. It certainly would be a lot more complex than he had imagined. The French could print the books, but they had to be delivered and then distributed.

"How many can you use?" asked Henri. What could he answer? True, the need for Christian literature was immeasurable but then so was the risk. Just one mistake and he would be whisked away in that black Volga. Vitali looked serious for a moment and then said, "Ivan Petrovich, don't worry. We already have a bit of experience doing this kind of thing." He glanced at his friend and then at the ceiling. "Let's go for a walk outside," Henri suggested.

Despite what had happened to him before, Vanya had never considered that his apartment might be bugged. He frowned at the oversight and showed the Frenchmen to the elevator.

Outside, it was still quite warm. They crossed into the park opposite and, when they were sure they were not being followed, began making arrangements for the delivery of a small consignment six months hence. Six months! How was this possible? In the Soviet Union it often took six years for a book to be published! They walked on, along avenues where old men wearing their medals played chess on the park benches and children made castles in the sand pits while their mothers watched and chattered to each other. The sun was already setting when Vanya led them to the tram stop and they bade farewell.

"Au revoir!" Vanya stammered, the only French he remembered. The doors closed, and they were gone.

With mixed feelings Vanya walked back to the apartment block. Six months! As he climbed into the elevator, he realized he had never been so happy. Also he had never been so afraid!

As it happened, the flat was not bugged. Six months later, Vanya met Henri a second time, on this occasion with his wife, whose Russian was about as good as Vanya's French. Things could not have gone more smoothly.

Over the next two years Vanya was visited several times by his foreign friends. Although it was pleasant for him to talk with his guests in the comfort of his own home, Vanya had decided that this was a risk which simply could not be taken. I noticed that whenever someone got out of the elevator, Anna Vasilyevna, our neighbor, would invariably peep out to see who it was. At first Vanya thought the old woman was just lonely and perhaps over-curious. A few weeks later, however, while talking to a couple of Henri's colleagues who had recently arrived in Moscow, there was a knock and no sooner had I opened the door than Anna Vasilyevna popped in the flat—for a loan of some matches, she said. Fortunately plenty of spare boxes were at hand so the inquisitive old lady had little opportunity to ask questions. We agreed that this was probably more than a coincidence, and that in all likelihood Anna Vasilyevna was being rewarded for keeping an eye on us.

From then on foreign guests could no longer come to

the apartment and meetings took place outside or in places without prying eyes. At each of these "meetings," precise arrangements had to be made for exactly when and where the next one would take place. Also contingency plans had to be made for second, third, and fourth meetings in the event of a hitch.

One thing which Vanya had not grasped at first was the enormity of distributing the books. First, he and his friends had to get time off from work which would coincide with the deliveries from abroad, so the problem of storage in Moscow would be minimized. Secondly, arrangements had to be made with their friends in the places where needs were the greatest. In order to plan these secondary deliveries, either they had to travel to the destination or their Christian brothers had to come to Moscow. To use the mails or the telephone was risky, and on those occasions on which there was no alternative, pre-arranged codes had to be used. Several times Vanya was reminded of an illegally copied James Bond film he had seen on a friend's video in Leningrad. But then he had only to remember what had happened to his old friends Volodya and Pasha or countless others to be convinced that all this security was necessary. The third major problem was that of actually delivering the literature.

Within a short while Vanya and his colleagues had driven several thousand miles along dreadful roads. In the USSR it is against the law to drive in a dirty car, but obeying that law is nearly impossible when confronted with the general standard of road surfaces. So if one is driving a long distance there is a risk of being stopped by the militia. If, however, a car is spotlessly clean, that too can attract the attention of the highway police. The wear and tear on Vanya's small car soon began to tell, and disaster struck when the engine finally gave out in the Ukraine—miles from anywhere. Try as he might, he could not get any spare parts and was forced to return home by train.

Vanya was constantly aware of the dangers involved in taking packages of Bibles across the USSR. The fear of arrest never left him. But whenever he saw the joy on the faces of Christians who, for the first time in their lives, had a Bible of their own, he knew the risks and anxiety and hours of prayer and planning were worthwhile. Nevertheless, he continued to be concerned about what could happen to his family if he were arrested. We could lose our home and possessions and be forced to live outside Moscow. The children might be deprived of the chance of a good higher education and a decent career. The Bible verses which had caused Vanya the most difficulty at that time were those which spoke about sacrificing everything, including one's family, for the sake of the gospel. I think no one can bring more honor to one's family than by putting Christ before everything else.

Whenever he could, Vanya went along to the cathedral to sing in the choir, often accompanied by Nadya and Misha. By now our daughter had grown into a tall young woman with her father's grey eyes and sharp features. Misha had taken after me and had fair hair and a rosy complexion. Both were committed Christians, and Misha, for his part, had already started thinking about the priesthood. First, however, he had to do his national service. His sister had decided to become a doctor and was now a medical student.

We had many close friends in the cathedral choir, and often after service our apartment would be filled with people enjoying fellowship and food. In the Orthodox Church the first Sunday service takes place on Saturday evening. (The new day is reckoned as beginning at sunset.)

One Saturday evening in the summer of 1985 we were having one of our "evenings," and as Vanya and a group of friends walked from the cathedral to the flat a fellow singer who had only recently started attending took his host aside and said he had an important matter to discuss with him. The man, whose name was Petya, said that he wanted to read a certain book and had been told that Vanya was the person to speak to. It was called *The Large Forest*—the book that Vanya himself had written. When Vanya asked who had recommended it, the other replied it was someone or other from Kolomna whose name he could not remember. Vanya could not remember having met anyone in recent years from that town. The number of people whom he had told about *The Large Forest* could be counted on the fingers of one hand.

All religious organizations in the Soviet Union are infiltrated by people for whom the interests of the state are more important than those of the gospel. From the bishops themselves down to the members of parish councils, thousands are in one way or another on the KGB payroll. Vanya suspected that Petya was one such person. He replied that he had heard of the book but that he did not possess a copy of it. After the meal Vanya accompanied Petya to the metro station.

A few weeks later Petya again approached Vanya and slipped a small book-shaped parcel into his hand. "I've read it and I'd like you to take it as a gift." Vanya thanked him and left the choir vestry and set off home. When he was sure that nobody was about he dropped his beloved book into a nearby rubbish bin. Misha and Nadya, who were with Vanya, looked at him first with amazement and then began to understand why he had done it. As they crossed the park Vanya put his greatest fears into words: The KGB was trying to find a pretext to arrest him, and when they want to do something there is nothing in the world which can stop them.

On 7 October 1985, ten-year-old Tanya came home from school and stepped out of the elevator to see a strange and terrifying sight. All the doors on our floor had been thrown wide open, including our own, and even more strange was that all the neighbors seemed to be in our flat. Amidst all the noise and commotion issuing from the kitchen little Tanya recognized the voice of our neighbor Anna Vasilyevna.

Tanya was very frightened. What was going on? If only her father hadn't gone to Kiev. At this time of day I would still be at work, and only Grandmother would be at home. She must get to her.

Quietly she slipped past the crowd in the kitchen and into the main room. On the sofa sat her grandmother, silently watching two policemen lifting things out of the cupboards and putting papers and letters into a box. Suddenly Tanya saw a third man who wasn't in police uniform standing and smoking on the balcony. The little girl stood in the doorway, not knowing what to do. All at once another man appeared from the kitchen and asked the others if they had found something or other. They said that they had searched everywhere. Then all four went onto the balcony and talked quietly to each other. The old woman smiled at Tanya and told her not to be frightened. A moment later the four men left, leaving Tanya and her grandmother alone. The little girl hadn't noticed the neighbors going. After all the noise and commotion, the silence seemed strange. Natalya Fyodorovna sighed deeply and crossed herself and told Tanya to help her clear up the mess before the rest of the family got home.

The ploy with the book had failed, but the KGB did not give up. A few days after his return from Kiev someone phoned Vanya and said that he needed to speak with him urgently. The voice was unknown. When Vanya asked what the problem was, the stranger refused to say, only adding that this was a matter of urgent concern and could seriously effect Vanya's family. At that moment the caller was waiting opposite the park in a small side street, a minute's walk from the apartment. Vanya rose from the table, crossed himself before the icons, kissed his family and went out.

It was two years before the children saw him again.

In May 1986, I sent the following letter to Henri in

Paris. It was addressed to all Christians and people of pure hearts and clear conscience:

> Beloved brothers and sisters in the Lord Jesus Christ, wherever you may be, we are appealing to you on behalf of Ivan Petrovich Pogodin (born 1944) who was arrested on the 16th of October 1985 in the Baumanskii District of Moscow and sentenced to five years strict regime camp labor with an additional five years internal exile under the Criminal Code of the RFSFR. The trial took place on January 3-7, 1986, under Moscow Procurator Dmitri Ivanovich Voloshin. We, his relatives, were told that the trial would take place at a later date and were only informed that the proceedings had begun on the second day, when my mother Natalya Fyodorovna Surikova, and myself, Irina Andreevna Pogodina, were called upon to testify in court. Also present was the brother of the accused, Konstantin Petrovich Pogodin.

> It was alleged that on the evening of the 16th of October 1985, I.P. Pogodin savagely attacked a defenseless man, one Pavel Antonovich Cherkasskii, who subsequently had to be taken to the hospital. The incident was observed by two law students, N.N. Lebedev and A.P. Sidorenko, both of whom happened to be in the vicinity at the time. They both testified against Ivan Pogodin. For his part, Ivan stated that he was not guilty and that it was Cherkasskii and another man who attacked him. He also claimed that he had not seen either Lebedev or Sidorenko before. We, the relatives and friends of Ivan Petrovich Pogodin, know him to be a peace-loving man. As his wife, I can say that in all the years I have known him, he has not once been violent. An important fact overlooked by the court is that as a result of an accident, there is no way that Ivan

Pogodin could strike another man in the way described by P.A. Cherkasskii.

Ivan Petrovich Pogodin was also accused of disseminating literature slanderous to the Soviet State. This he also denied, saying in his defense that the court could not consider the Bible as being slanderous since the government of the USSR allowed certain religious organizations to print them and even import them. Regarding his own literary works the court must have misunderstood his two books if they considered them slanderous. Evidence was also produced showing that the accused had extensive connections with foreigners "and therefore with anti-Soviet organizations."

From his arrest to the time of the trial and for a short time after being accused, Ivan Pogodin was held in the Lefortovo Prison in Moscow. He was then sent to the camp, the address of which has not yet been released.

Dear brothers and sisters, we ask you to do everything you can in praying and working with us for the release of Ivan Pogodin, whose crime has been that he loves the Lord Jesus Christ and has tried to fulfill the commandments of the holy gospel to proclaim the Good News of Truth to all men.

Signed,

Irina Andreevna Pogodina
Natalya Fyodorovna Surikova
Nadezhda Ivanovna Pogodina
Mikhail Ivanovich Pogodin
Konstantin Petrovich Pogodin
Lyudmila Denisovna Smirnova
Alexander Timofeyovich Vygodskii
Alexander Alexandrovich Mauer
Maria Konstantinovna Mauer
Vasily Alexandrovich Mauer

Vanya was taken first to Vladimir, a town to the east of Moscow and the site of an infamous transit prison. From there he traveled the long journey across Siberia, finally to be detained in a large, strict regime camp not far from Blagoveshchensk, near the Chinese border. It was from here that I received the first of Vanya's letters. He wrote that, thanks to the prayers of his brothers and sisters, he was in good health and spirits, and was now almost fully recovered after his illness. (This was the first we had heard about Vanya falling sick en route from Vladimir.) All camp mail is strictly censored so he could be specific about little.

In the autumn of 1986 I made the long journey to the camp. Not only was this physically difficult but it was also expensive. Since the trial I had been dismissed from work and was now working as a cleaner in a factory. In order to visit Vanya it had been necessary to borrow a considerable sum of money from friends. When I finally reached the camp, the administrator's secretary told me that my husband had been transferred to a different camp and that I should have been informed about this by the Ministry. But no letter had been or subsequently was received. Regarding the new destination, the secretary said that I would be presently informed, but at this stage it would be an infringement of the rules to disclose the address of the new camp. I therefore had to make the arduous journey back home. I later learned that Vanya had been sent to Angara, a town near to Irkutsk. To add to the irony, on my return journey I had become ill with what was later to develop into pneumonia, and had been compelled to spend four days with distant relatives in Irkutsk!

Things were certainly grim both for Vanya who, despite his bad arm, was forced to do the same amount of arduous manual labor as the rest of the inmates, and for me, since my illness had resulted in losing the cleaning job and its meager income. Vanya claimed that had it not been for God's sustaining power and the knowledge that people were praying for him, he would have gone under. My pneumonia had been much more serious than at first had been thought, and I was later amazed at how near to death and total despair I had been. Our son Misha during this time had been called up to do his national service and was away in the army. He suffered greatly for his faith there but came through the test well, standing up for Christ with courage.

Our situation finally got better as *glasnost* became more than talk. Amnesty was declared for a large number of political prisoners, and among those to be released was Vanya Pogodin. Technically speaking, the word amnesty was a misnomer; in order to be released the prisoner had to sign a document in which he admitted that the act for which he had been charged was wrong and to promise not to engage in such things again. The precise wording of these papers differed; for some it amounted to a confession of guilt, and some such as Vladimir Rusak bravely refused to sign and are now continuing their sentences.[1] For others, the wording was more vague and one could sign the document without an act of moral compromise. All Vanya had to do was to state that malicious hooliganism and propagating dangerous literature were wrong and that he would not engage in either in the future.

In the summer of 1987, Vanya returned to Moscow and has been given back his old job. I work part-time at a printing plant. Our faith is as strong as ever. We give thanks to God for our many blessings.

Notes

1. Vladimir Rusak has since been released and has emigrated from the Soviet Union.

CHAPTER 16

STANDING STRONG
DESPITE OPPOSITION
by Tibor Lanyi

*Introduction: Christianity in the region of
modern Hungary began in the third century,
spreading from the Roman Empire. Both
Lutheran and Calvinist forms of the Reformation
reached the area and have their continuing
influence, although Catholicism remains the
dominant form of Christian faith. Typically of
the east European Communist countries, the
constitution guarantees religious liberty; also
typically the reality has been far different.
Wholesale repression of the churches became
common after 1948, but there was nothing like
the periodic attempts in the Soviet Union to wipe
out religious expression entirely. Rather, the
government sought to control church leadership.
This manipulation was often successful; when it
was not, pastors who insisted on maintaining the*

integrity of the church went to prison. Some were put to death. There has been much suffering in the church since 1949.

Of all the changes that have taken place in eastern Europe, perhaps nowhere have they been so comprehensive as those in Hungary. Even in the short period since Tibor Lanyi told this story there has been a revolution there, although of a peaceful sort. The Communist party has actually disbanded itself and re-formed as a socialist party. Many Hungarian churchmen now say that religious repression is gone from the land. How long-lasting this situation will be is impossible to say, but a return to the old system seems highly unlikely; so disastrous was it for Hungary that almost nobody favors it.

Pastor Lanyi has asked us not to reveal the identity of his denomination.

• • •

When we arrived here five years ago we looked around and saw problems in the church. State discrimination had bred a spirit of fear among the people. They regarded government officials as the Caesars of the village, all-powerful in the lives of their children. Officials used their positions to control not only children but also adults. Everyone understood that if parents displeased the officials, punishment would fall on the heads of the children, who could then say goodbye to further educational opportunity. It is strange how small villages like ours can have committed ideologues and Stalinists in sensitive positions. They act as if it were still 1956 when Soviet tanks crushed our nation's push for democracy and put hardliners into power.

At the time of our arrival the church met in a beautiful old structure dating from the late eighteenth century. It sits on the top of a hill, its high tower dominating the village. You can see it from anywhere in the vicinity. It has always moved me to watch people walking up the path to church on a Sunday morning, like a river flowing in its channel. Still, the building was far from adequate, and we have recently finished another facility. We still use the old building, but the new one is much warmer in the winter and has better facilities for special meetings, especially for children. Before we built it we held children's meetings in the basement of our home, sometimes with one hundred boys and girls jammed into a small room.

Young people in our church are divided into separate groups for small children (ages 4-10), children (10-14), and youth (14-23). Our regular confirmation classes are a problem because for many people they are simply a tradition with no meaning. Out of nine who were confirmed last year, only one has continued with the youth group. Most of the active and faithful members of the group are from non-religious families who do not bring their children forward for confirmation class. From these experiences I have decided not to confirm children who do not give evidence of faith in Christ, regardless of the pressures parents bring to bear.

Many of the youth, however, have a deep and mature faith. Those who are still in school use their school holidays to travel together to a home for severely mentally and physically handicapped children to do volunteer work there for a week or two. This work is difficult but beautiful because the handicapped children so need to be loved. Sometimes we take all our children to visit similar groups in other churches in order to encourage them.

Early in my ministry I concentrated a lot on children. My wife, Eva, has a strong interest in and gift for working with children. Gradually she took over this side of our ministry. She was much helped by a correspondence course from the Theological Academy. After she completed the course, church leaders allowed her to work with the children.

Eva's successful work attracted many children, and some people did not appreciate this. Now Eva leads the Sunday school and three children's groups. She uses flannelgraphs, stories, Scripture memory, and songs to teach the children about Jesus. She has to work very hard to make these groups successful, partly because it is impossible to get the materials she needs. For example, we received one copy of a course on the person of Jesus Christ for use with a whole group. She typed the course sixteen times so that each member of the group could have one. Our daughter now says, "Whenever I see my mother she is typing, always typing."

We allow none of this to discourage us. Children are of great importance to our ministry. What happens to the church in the future depends to a large degree on how well we teach children now. Of course, the Communist regime fully agrees with us; that is why they have devoted so much effort to indoctrinate the young ones in Marxist dogma. So there is a natural conflict between what the children learn in church and what they learn in school.

The conflict differs from school to school. In our village the elementary level is toughest. Faculty competency is low; teachers have little or no training in the subjects they are supposed to teach. Their training is largely in Communist party doctrine, and their appointments were made on the basis of their competence in that field. They discriminate regularly against children who are believers. Included in the lessons are many false statements that almost any educated person could expose easily. But children are often not able to see that they are being taught lies.

In an effort to turn the children of believers away from the faith, some teachers are not satisfied merely to teach materialism. They also ridicule the children. In one class, the wife of the school headmaster (who is also the party secretary) asked the children to raise their hands if they believed in God. Then she said to them in front of

the whole class: "Why are you believers? Christianity is a
false doctrine that no modern person could believe.
Where is God? If God exists, the cosmonauts would have
seen him." In spite of the hostility many of the Christian
children gave good answers to these provocations.

Our own children were special targets of this
discrimination. When we first moved here my son's name
always appeared on the Friday afternoon reports as
having misbehaved that week. One time he stayed home
for a whole week with a broken wrist, and on Friday we
found that he still made the weekly list of bad boys. He
was about six or seven years old at the time. Both he and
my younger daughter were mocked in the school.

Suzie is a quiet child, and when something bothers
her she withdraws within herself. These teachers knew
that and used it as a weapon against her. They would
often mock her openly in front of the class in order to
harm her psychologically. They would deliberately ask
her questions they knew she could not answer. And then
they would say, "Ah yes, Suzie, we should have known it
was you. No wonder there is no answer." It would
happen daily, in mathematics, Russian, and other
subjects. And then they would make fun of her. She
suffered greatly from this stress, which often gave her
stomachaches. Each morning she was afraid to go to
school. And she was far from the only one. The other
girls from the church youth group also would cry when
they saw how the teachers mistreated Suzie.

The children all knew that it was our youth work that
made school authorities so angry and led to their troubles
in class. But nobody asked us to please the authorities by
stopping the work.

The headmaster and his wife have made the
educational situation in our village intolerable. If a child
wants to study further after elementary school they make
it difficult or impossible to go on by giving lower grades
than the child deserves. They also report to the high
school authorities that these are the children of believers.

The children know what is happening, and when they reach the seventh grade, the one just before high school, some stop coming to the various church functions. Of course, this is just what the atheist school officials desired all along!

I often preached about this and urged the people not to be afraid but to rely on the Lord's care and protection. As a result of this teaching—which is nothing more than ancient Christian doctrine, although it is often forgotten by the church—many people have become active in living the Christian faith. They realize that ultimately the power of these teachers is nothing, and that the effects of their work can be overcome.

When parents began complaining to the party office about the teachers, it did no good. The party was especially disinclined to help people connected with our church because of the embarrassment we caused them. During our first summer in the village we organized a camp for children, and sixty-eight boys and girls showed up. Sixty-eight children in a Christian camp! What a disaster for the public relations effort of the local party. Tattletales ran to the party office complaining that the pastor had directed the children to read the Bible and pray and other such things.

A policeman came to the church from the party office to discuss this problem with me. I showed him no fear and said that I had done similar things in previous places where I had ministered. How strange that it was a problem here but not in those other towns! I explained that only wholesome things took place in the camp and that both the children and the parents liked what we were doing there. "I am very surprised that in these times when young people so often get into trouble, it becomes a problem for the party and for the school teachers that we teach children to live upright lives," I said. I mentioned that the headmaster's wife had rejoiced in the filthy language used by her young grandchild and contrasted that with the way the church urged parents to raise their children. And I asked him to judge for himself which was better for the children and for the country.

When he left, the policeman said quietly: "What you are doing is good. I can see the children you are training are turning out well. I wish you continued success in your work."

But the struggle was far from over. As the church became increasingly active, the hostility of the schoolmaster and his wife also increased. They made many trips to the county party office to report the activities of the church, and especially the thriving young people's group. But party officials were not inclined to do anything about it. Sometimes they even said we were a good influence on the community.

Increasingly we found that, by no coincidence, the school was scheduling special mandatory programs at the same time our church youth were to meet. This placed great pressure on our young people.

Still, we have many opportunities for service and for witnessing to the faith. One of the girls in our youth group got very sick in the hospital not long ago. She received many letters from the young people. Others in the hospital could see how many people really cared for this girl. She read her Bible regularly and had an effect on the doctors and nurses. Another girl is away at school, living in a dormitory. After the official "lights out" she left her light on to read the Bible. A teacher saw the light and came to investigate. When she saw the Bible she was very interested. They now meet regularly to discuss the Bible.

This interest and openness in spiritual things is quite new for Hungary, something not true everywhere in eastern Europe. Great changes are taking place in this part of the world. The church needs to prepare to take advantage of these changes. God is hearing and answering prayers. Believers are no longer afraid as they were a few years ago.

Often we find that our difficulties come as much from

our church's denomination as from the state. This became clear when we began planning for our new building. Village elections were instituted about that time, and local officials were not anxious to give us any trouble. But the church bureaucracy was another story. First I had to get permission from the village government, then the deacon's office, the bishop's office, the county office, and the state office in Budapest. All these steps presented some difficulties. The deacons were on vacation; the county officer was ill; we had to wait for a meeting of the county leaders; the bishop was abroad. But eventually we got the signatures we needed. I believe church officials dragged their feet because of pressure from government and party officials. That is typical in the relationship of church and state in Hungary.

Once we had the license to build, the congregation really pitched in. We laid the foundation in only three days, and in another three the walls were up. People volunteered their services when they could. We never asked anyone for help except our own people. All we said from the pulpit was: "If anyone has time and skill to offer, your help would be welcome." And they came and gave and worked. They were able to use their skills for God's glory. The church was built in about three years by this small army of dedicated believers working in their spare time.

Our progress did not please everyone in the hierarchy. Central church authorities are especially reluctant about people in the provinces accomplishing anything without their help and direction. They sent subtle messages intended to discourage us from the job; an official never seemed to be in when we called, simple questions rarely got straight answers, and files disappeared. Some people in our congregation doubted we would be able to overcome all these obstacles. It reminded us of Nehemiah and those who opposed his plan to rebuild Jerusalem's walls. But the walls were built!

Our own story has a happier ending than we had

expected. By the time of the elections, villagers had a good chance to see what the headmaster and his wife were trying to do to the church and its youth. When the ballots were counted, our two adversaries lost their local offices. This was a major defeat for them and a great encouragement to the believers in the village.

CHAPTER 17

THE FILE
by Maria Cerny

*Introduction: The history of central and
eastern Europe is difficult to grasp. The common
western experience of stable frontiers over long
periods of time is unknown there. Whole countries
disappear for a time, then come to life again, then
are divided up once more. Nations seldom
coincide with state boundaries. Within
Czechoslovakia, for example, people speak not
only the two major languages—Czech and
Slovak—but also Hungarian, Romany, Russian,
German, Polish, Ukrainian, and other tongues.*

*In common with most of eastern Europe,
Czechoslovakia was swept into the Communist
orbit after World War II. From 1948, when a coup
brought in Communist rule, until only a few
months ago, this former democracy with a
thriving industrial economy has suffered the*

maladies endemic to Communist states: political and religious repression and economic weakness (although the country remains wealthier than most of the others). Add to that the demoralization that accompanies them.

Roman Catholicism is the dominant form of Christianity in Czechoslovakia, although a number of smaller Protestant denominations exist. No doubt mindful of the difficulties Catholics caused for the Communist government of Poland, just to the north, the Czechoslovak authorities have been much harder on the Catholic church than on the Protestants. The government was much stricter about literature access for Catholics than for others. For example, parishioners of a particular Catholic church in Prague have been unable to obtain Bibles in their church, but could buy them from a Baptist church across the street. Until the recent democratic revolution, most of the bishoprics in the country were vacant because the government and the Vatican could not agree on who should occupy those positions. The Communist regime would agree only to appoint those priests willing to take orders from the politicians.

After much initial uncertainty, the new winds blowing through the Soviet Union and some of its allies blew past the guard thrown up by a frightened but determined Czechoslovak Communist party. A Roman Catholic is now president of the country, and there is little prospect that the Communists will again be able to put the lid on.

Still, among the lessons we should have learned from the recent turmoil is that the unexpected can always happen. Maria Cerney tells us in this chapter of the central importance of the file *in administering a totalitarian state.*

Where are those files now, and what use will be made of them in the future?

• • •

Outsiders who wish to understand how we live must grasp the central idea of the *file*. Whoever we are, whatever we do, and wherever we go, the file goes with us. It tells the reader almost everything he wants to know about us. And the main thing he wants to know is how reliable we are politically. School, work, military service, information about our parents and our upbringing—whatever we have done, how we did it, the nature of our political convictions—everything is in the file.

We are not allowed to see the file. But every year each employer makes an entry. He calls us in to read the entry, and both of us sign it. Then into the file it goes. If we think the manager has been unfair in making the entry we can appeal it through our union. The union, however, is called the Worker's Revolutionary Movement, and since it is controlled by the Communist party—which also controls the enterprise in which we work—the appeal cannot be taken seriously.

In spite of the rule about not seeing your own file, my sister and I have seen ours. Our employers were either especially friendly or had no particular respect for the regime and its ideology.

My sister's file says our father is a fanatical Christian. Someone from our village wrote to the school which employed her and asked, "How is it possible to employ a Christian in a place like that?" She was an assistant at the university, a very sensitive position, and immediately the administration wanted to fire her. Fortunately, she was pregnant at the time, and the rules forbade her dismissal. Instead she was allowed to stay home for three years. When she returned to the university they confronted her with the letter and asked, "Is this true? Are you a Christian?" She answered, "Yes, I am." So they dismissed her and ended her career. This letter is still in her file and will stay there for the rest of her life.

My own file contained a similar letter, but my supervisor was a secret believer. She had been a partisan in the war and therefore was given a high position. But to keep it she must avoid going to church. My position would be hopelessly out of reach if this woman had not protected me. The notation in my file that I am a Christian would have kept me from all but the simplest kind of work.

My supervisor's action is quite common. Solidarity among the people keeps the party directives from being implemented to their full extent. Of course, this is not universal; plenty of officials take delight in denying justice to believers or to anyone who is not a member of their little circle of friends and supporters. It is rule by clique.

Information for the file can come from almost any source. Children are frequently used to gather information on their parents. A child writes in a school exercise that his parents go to church, and that information finds its way into the parents' files. Theoretically it is not permitted to write about religion in the file but it happens anyway. Sometimes such information is turned over to the secret police, which uses it to blackmail the parents to work as informers.

Our children must go to school for ten years, starting at age six. Kindergarten comes before that, for ages three to five, but there aren't enough places for all the children. So only those whose mothers work are allowed to go to kindergarten. Before kindergarten there is child care for children between the ages of six months and three years. The basic school runs from ages six to fourteen. Then we have the higher school for two to three years. Higher education or technical school follows for a certain percentage of the young people.

For the most part we mothers have no choice about whether to work; we cannot buy sufficient food and clothing if we do not work. It is disheartening to see droves of twenty-year-old mothers taking children to kindergarten at 6 A.M., or even 5, because they must be on the job at 6:30. The buses are so full that many people cannot get on, and they have to wait in the cold for the next one. It is the same between 3 and 6 in the evening when the children come home from kindergarten. Some have been there all day, and the buses are full of crying children. In the winter it is especially bad.

This situation is generally true only in the large towns. In the villages and small towns the extended family is more normal, and the grandparents look after the children. One factor has been a big help to young families. Mothers have the option of taking three years at home after a child is born; the first two years are with pay, and the third can be taken as an option. They are guaranteed their jobs when they return. Many Christian women take this opportunity to rear their children. Otherwise the child has to go to an infant care center and is denied mother's love even in the first years of its life.

We live in a large town. In one area 100,000 people live in large blocks of apartments. Everyone goes to work by bus because it is so expensive to run cars. Even those who have them don't use them for commuting. So from our part of town, 50,000 people jam into the buses twice a day going to and from work.

When I was pregnant with the first of my three children, I told my supervisor I would be taking the three years off. He threatened me with the loss of my job if I tried to do the same thing with another child, despite the legal guarantees. When the mother cannot take the time from work, it leads to many problems in the family.

Our family, like almost all in Czechoslovakia, cannot live on one income. If the mother stays home, the man has to take two jobs or else will have to go back to clean up the offices after hours. There have been enough jobs to go around, but the work is very unsatisfactory. There seems to be little to do and with morale generally low there is no incentive to improve your efforts. I can do all of my work in three or four hours a day and even if I wanted to, I would not be able to find more work. So while we do not have any unemployment to speak of, there is a kind of chronic underemployment.

Our country is officially classless, as are all those based on the teachings of Marxism-Leninism. Yet there is a group of people we call the "Upper Ten Thousand" who live differently than the rest. These people are the highest members of the Communist party and their relatives. A few are famous artists or scientists, but for the most part politics is the profession that gets people into this privileged class.

This is hidden by the way in which salaries are paid. My salary, for example, is 3,000 crowns [$317] a month. My director is paid 5,900 crowns [$624], but his total income last year was 200,000 crowns [$21,164]. The ministry pays him a bonus, or premium, based on whether he does his job in the way the ministry desires. So the system allows the privileged class to enjoy its benefits while using the bonus as a lever to get people to behave in desirable ways.

In our system the extra money does little good, however, because of an enormous shortage of goods and services. To deal with this problem there exist special stores in which only the Upper 10,000 are permitted to shop. There are also clinics and hospitals set aside for their use alone.

It is often difficult to obtain medicines in Czechoslovakia which are common in other countries. Not long ago I tried to help a friend whose daughter had an eye ailment. She needed a particular kind of medication unobtainable from the usual sources. I spoke to a pharmacist who told me that only the Upper 10,000 could get the product. As a last resort I went to the export-import office and asked them about it. They told me that only three bottles of that medicine had been imported during the entire year, although it is very common and cheap in the West. While this was being explained to me, the pharmacist from the special clinic for the Upper 10,000 came in. She was gracious enough to give me some of the medication. She said it is very common and cheap, but for some reason we do not import much of it or make it ourselves.

These shortages affect the way we obtain the most common of our needs. After work we go to three or four shops just for things of everyday use. One shop may have no bread; another may be out of flour or sugar. It is odd, but with all this difficulty the shops appear to be well stocked. We have a saying that the shops are always full but not with anything you want. Everything comes in waves. Suddenly there will be children's clothing (perhaps of a certain size only), and then later there will be no children's clothing. Then there will be books or maybe shoes, and soon they will disappear. The way we deal with this is to buy whatever comes on the market if we think we'll need it later on. All this comes from bad distribution, and it leads to panic buying and false shortages. Last summer we could not get any sandals for our youngest daughter. But then someone got them in another town.

We come home exhausted at the end of the day. We are always under great time pressure because it takes so long to get what we need. The time we would like to give to church work and our children instead goes into maintaining the household. Parents leave work, go home, make and eat the evening meal, and put the children to bed. No energy remains for anything more.

These difficulties are worsened by the serious shortage of housing. Although there are several ways to get an apartment, they all require long waiting periods, sometimes as much as ten years. You pay a certain percentage of the purchase price and then wait until a place becomes available. Company housing also exists.

You agree to stay with a company for so many years, and then it allocates an apartment for you. The situation is so tight that sometimes divorced persons have to live in the same apartment with the new spouse of the divorced partner. Several homes for single adults are like dormitories. Many people will live in a room and share a bathroom and kitchen with similar groups in other rooms on the same corridor.

It is sometimes possible to exchange your apartment for a larger one if you can find a divorced couple looking for other accommodations. This can be extremely time-consuming as well as expensive. Our ordeal began when we decided to have my mother move in with us after she had become too frail to care for herself. We thought that if we could exchange the two apartments for one larger one we would be able to keep her with us. In our society the extended family is very important. Our apartment was seventy-six square meters for five of us, and my mother's was sixty square meters. To find the apartment we placed numerous newspaper advertisements, each one costing one hundred crowns [$10.68], about a day's pay. Then came numerous telephone calls and visits. Once we found the right place the paperwork began.

We found a few modern apartments with five rooms, but the rooms were so small we wouldn't have gained anything. Once we found the place we wanted and agreed to terms, we began our duel of patience with the bureaucracy. We had to fill out sixteen forms for each member of the family and for each apartment that was being exchanged. Several times they returned our papers supposedly because of mistakes we had made. But there were no errors. They could not understand how three apartments could be exchanged. When our papers finally were accepted, they had to be sent to a higher office for approval. Then each of us, including all the children, had to attend the official signing. Everyone must be present to prove that they exist. Then approval must come from the three institutes which own the apartments. Then the town hall. We still do not have all the approvals and are hoping that some time in the future we can move.

The teaching of atheism comes in every form and at every level. Beginning in kindergarten and continuing through the most advanced training, the root ideas of materialism are drilled into the people. It is understood that if you want to get ahead, you give the teachers and officials the answers they want. We all say what is expected regardless of what we believe.

This raises a serious problem for Christians. What do we tell our children? We told our daughter that she must study what the teachers require and she must give them the answers they want, even if she does not believe them. That's the way we prepare our children for this double life. When someone writes or says what he really believes, he is put under enormous pressure. A student may not be allowed to take his final exams or may have to repeat a year of school. Or an exam that he passed suddenly has its grade changed to failing.

The higher the level of education, the more difficult it becomes to tell the truth. In my school we had a girl who spoke her mind about the system. Her professor was a secret believer and helped her. The authorities wanted to throw her out but the professor asked for six months to work with her and convince the girl of her error. Privately she told the girl not to talk about her faith but rather to adopt the role of secret believer. This was her final year of school, and she was able to finish her course of studies only because this secret believer intervened.

In the lower grades the schools teach more about Marxism and evolution than they do atheism. As the children get older they come to a part of the curriculum called "The Citizen's Lesson." Here they learn the history of the state and the organization of the party. They are taught to have a high regard for the military and the police. They take field trips to police stations, stroke the police dogs, and visit the border guards. They learn that the barbed wire at the frontier protects the nation against enemies living on the other side. And it is drilled into them that if they observe anything taking place that opposes the state, they must report it to the authorities.

Children are not asked if they wish to join the Communist youth movement, nor are their parents. They are put on the rolls automatically. They meet once a week after school and are required to take part in the activities. During the first two years of school they are called "Sparks" and do little more than play together. Between the third and eighth years of school they join the "Pioneers," or socialist club. Sports continue during this period, but a heavy dose of cultural and political content is added. Children are taught to be watchful and to report any suspicious activities. By the time students reach university age, the principles of atheism have been drilled into them.

During state visits by high dignitaries, such as Brezhnev, we must go out into the streets to give a welcome. In some factories workers had to sign a statement saying they were actually at the demonstration.

It is different with Gorbachev. The Czechoslovak leaders—old-fashioned Communists uncomfortable with shows of democracy—are afraid that the Soviet leader will try to meet the people, so only a few are forced to be on hand to greet him. Perhaps that is part of the reason why the big Communist holidays, such as May Day, are much more restrained than they used to be.

Since religion has been so much a part of our culture for centuries, it is impossible for the atheist state to ignore it. The task for authorities is to explain away something that is impressed upon our language, our architecture, our music, and almost every other part of our culture. The textbooks explain that belief in God stems from a time when science was not as advanced as it is now, when people were afraid of what they could not explain. But now that science has explained everything, the need for religion is gone.

One problem with this "explanation" is that it doesn't reveal why there are so many demonstrations, attracting thousands of modern people, on behalf of the persecuted church. Therefore the authorities have a second lie to account for this inconvenient fact. They say that the modern church is a tool in the hand of western ideology which uses religion to bring us back to the slavery of capitalism.

Living under these conditions forces us to teach our children how to cope with a kind of schizophrenia. We all suffer it from time to time. From the earliest days our children learn how to live at the same time in a Christian family and a world that is officially atheist—and which bombards them with the idea that their family is backward and ignorant. Thus our life is preoccupied with survival. For the most part we cannot get by if we live as though wearing a badge that says "I am a Christian." We may go to church but say little of it. We try to live our life as Christians but without much verbal witness. If we were to preach openly or do the sort of evangelism that perhaps we should, we would become like Stephen in the Book of Acts, who was stoned.

Our evangelism has to be done solely through personal contacts. If I speak to a friend about faith in Christ he will not report this to the secret police. But I have to make sure he is really a friend before I say a word. If I start a new job and say I'm a Christian, people will have nothing to do with me out of fear. Not long ago a man in our organization died. His funeral was in a church and for that reason the directors forbade any Communist party members from attending. The party expects that none of its members set foot in a church.

Still, it is widely known that many have joined the party only for career reasons and that some are secret believers. Others want their children to be baptized or want to be married in the church. To do this they will often go to a village many miles away where they are not known. Or they may attend regular services in that way.

It is all part of the schizophrenia that comes from superimposing an atheistic system on what was once a Christian country. One of my favorite illustrations of our culture's split personality is found on the cover page of my Bible. It says:

Holy Bible
Publishing House of the Communist Party

The Bible was printed on the Communist presses during what we know as the "Prague Spring," a brief period in the 1960s when the Dubcek regime liberalized many aspects of our lives—until the experiment was crushed by Soviet tanks.

Similar ironies happen all the time because of society's complete corruption. Some time ago the police were furious when they discovered that Christian tracts had been printed on party presses. Someone paid the official printer to do it. Money will buy almost any illegal product or service here, and often it is officials who do the selling.

This year a mass meeting of Roman Catholics in Bratislava protested the way the state dealt with the church. The state banned the demonstration, which was to take place outside the opera house. Academic officials told students that if they attended the demonstration, they would be expelled. The boarding house for university students was closed, and the residents were sent home. Younger students with parents known to be religious were called in and intimidated. Workers were told that if they attended the demonstration, they would lose their jobs. On the very day of the protest the government announced that there would be roadwork in the area.[1]

The great consolation for followers of Christ in my country is that there is a file in heaven which is just. It does not depend on bosses or politicians, and it will remain after all those other files, which now seem so important, are gone.

Notes

1. On March 25, 1988, about two thousand people gathered in Bratislava, the capital of the eastern Czechoslovak region of Slovakia, in spite of the government ban against the demonstration. The crowd stood in front of the National Theater, motivated by the desire for religious liberty. It was a protest mainly against the failure of the state to approve the appointment of a new bishop since the post was vacated in 1973. Of the thirteen bishoprics in the country, ten were vacant, with the remaining three occupied by men more than seventy-five years of age. The police arrested several hundred demonstrators after beating many of them severely (*New York Times*, 27 March 1988).

CHAPTER 18

THE PASTOR
AND THE COMMITTEE
by Hristo Hristov Kulichev

Introduction: Bulgaria, a small nation on the Black Sea, has been part of the violent history for which the Balkans have been known for centuries. Conflicting pressures come from Romania and the Soviet Union to the north, Yugoslavia to the west, and Greece and Turkey to the South. When the Soviet Union imposed its ideology throughout eastern Europe at the end of World War II, Bulgaria fell under Communist control. Alone of the Communist bloc peoples, the Bulgarians apparently have a high regard and appreciation for the Russians. This stems partly from their common Slavic culture and language (both use the Cyrillic alphabet, for example) but also from historical circumstances. Bulgaria had been dominated by the Turks for almost half a millennium when it revolted in 1876. Imperial

Russia was a source of aid in this successful overthrow of the oppressors. The Bulgarians' gratitude to the Russians extended through the Communist revolution and exists in some measure today.

Christianity has existed in the area of modern Bulgaria since the second century. In common with much of eastern Europe, Orthodox Christianity is the form that has dominated the country. There are also Roman Catholics in Bulgaria, and in the mid-nineteenth century Protestantism began to flourish in small pockets.

As in the rest of the Communist world, the official state teaching, atheism, until recently, dominated education at all levels. In Bulgaria there is apparently less disenchantment with the ideology of the state than elsewhere. This made it more difficult for Bulgarian Christians because the hostility of the authorities is matched by that of many people around them.

But beyond ideology there is always the question of power. The church and the family both have legitimate spheres of authority, and totalitarian governments do not recognize any authority but their own. Who is responsible for placing pastors in churches, the members or the state? Who is responsible for rearing children, the parents or the state? The differing answers to these questions set the stage for the conflicts in which Bulgarian Christians find themselves and the kind of dilemmas they face in making decisions.

A lot of history preceded Pastor Kulichev's entry into prison. The Communist regime wasted little time in putting its foot on the neck of the church after it took over at the end of World War II. It conducted a mass trial of a number of Baptist, Congregationalist, Pentecostal, and Methodist pastors in 1949. The charge was espionage. Even before that the Roman Catholics had suffered a similar fate. These were all trumped-up charges intended to make the churches subservient to the wishes of the ruling political forces.

Pastor Kulichev was not immune from these troubles. A university graduate in literature, he had become a teacher. But the school dismissed him because he was a Christian and preached in a church. He then entered the building trades, but after sixteen years in that occupation was again fired, for the same reason. Through all this he continued to serve the church as a preacher.[1]

The vast changes occurring in eastern Europe in late 1989 have not left Bulgaria untouched. But the revolution there is less far-reaching than in other countries, and as this is written it is not yet clear whether a democratic regime will emerge from the ruins of communism.

• • •

On January 9, 1985, the iron door of cell number seventy-four closed behind me. I put my sleeping pallet beside those of my two cellmates and made ready for a long and uncomfortable stay. My place was closest to the cell door, right next to the toilet bucket—that is always the lot of the newcomer. Naturally, when a place in the cell opens up everyone moves as far away from the odors as possible, so the newcomer ends up in the only place remaining.

This all began when the leader of our church, Pastor Bojovaiski, retired because of his advanced age. In our church pastors are elected by a vote of the people, and the congregation selected me to succeed him as pastor. But to everyone's amazement, a man named Pavel Ivanov showed up in church one day and announced that *he* was the new pastor. His justification was that "the

Committee sent me." By this he meant the committee appointed by the Ministry of the Interior to oversee the churches.

Nobody in the church expected Ivanov to show up as he did. It was unthinkable that we would turn the pulpit over to a man who did not serve the church in the name of God, but in the name of the Committee. It reminded me of the words in the Gospel of John which speak of John the Baptist: "There was a man who was sent from God; his name was John" (John 1:6). Of Pavel Ivanov one could say, "There was a man sent by the Committee." Can a man like this preach in the name of the Lord?

Representatives of our church held several meetings with the head of this Committee—a man by the name of Cvetkov—in order to resolve the issue. But Cvetkov persisted in his demand that I withdraw voluntarily. He was hoping that the Committee's pressure on the church would not be visible to outsiders, especially abroad.

With that avenue blocked, we had a four-hour discussion with the acting city prosecutor. There, various means of pressure were placed on us. The prosecutor brought up the question of what part I might have played in the events that led to the pastors' trial in 1949. He showed me a copy of article 324 of the statutes. This referred to persons who exercised a profession without authorization, and it carried a penalty of a year of imprisonment.

Along with the stick the prosecutor offered a carrot: He said they would help me find other work if I would step down and clear the way for Pavel Ivanov. He maintained that since I did not have the approval of the Committee, it was not legal for me to work as a pastor. I insisted that in conformity with Bulgarian law concerning religion, it was not necessary for me to have the Committee's approval. According to article 9, those who serve a church which has relations with overseas organizations need the approval of the Committee. But the Bulgarian Congregational Church is completely independent and has no foreign ties. Our custom is to grant the right to preach to anyone called by the church.

The prosecutor then pointed to article 10 of the law which requires a pastor to have good moral qualities, implying that I was disqualified. I responded with two statements. The first was that there had been no written communication that had taken from me the right to act as a pastor. And second, nobody had ever suggested anything I had done which might violate the legal requirements of moral behavior. Thus, no basis existed for saying I did not have the right to be a pastor. This long conversation turned out to be a series of moves and counter-moves:

Prosecutor: Suppose there are facts which cannot be communicated because the national interest will not permit it.

Kulichev: I cannot accept that anyone is obliged to hide dishonesty under the pretext of national interest, and especially in the case of someone like me who has become troublesome to the authorities. There is nothing easier than unmasking dishonesty.

Prosecutor: You must understand that in no case will the Committee agree to your continuing as pastor of the First Congregational Church.

Kulichev: You express the point of view of the Committee. But tell me, what I can do with this little word—*duty?* This word is deeply impressed into me. I believe that anyone who refuses to do his duty is unworthy of respect, and the one who shirks his duty in order to please others acts dishonestly.

Prosecutor: And your duty requires that you serve here in Sofia no matter what it costs you?

Kulichev: No, not at all. The place and manner in which I serve God is not important. Nor is the title and position.

Prosecutor: In that case, you could remain in the church and work in the same way you did with

Bojovaiski while another person holds the title of pastor. Will you agree to that? I understand that you do not want to work with Pavel Ivanov. But with another . . . ?

Kulichev: The issue is not who is pastor, but whether the choice is in accord with the legitimate rights of the church. It is the church that chooses its servants. Whomever it chooses—even Pavel Ivanov—I am obliged to submit myself to its decision. Whether I would work with him is another question, but I would accept the decision of the church whatever it might be. And since the church has chosen me for this work, I have to accomplish my duty as pastor.

Prosecutor: I have to tell you frankly that a trial would be an extremely unfortunate matter for you and for your family. But it would also be undesirable for the government because word of what is happening here usually spreads to international circles.

Kulichev: We are not the ones bringing this trouble to pass. We are only asking to live our spiritual lives in peace. We have not caused a problem for anyone. We are having this problem only because Mr. Cvetkov is trying to impose Pavel Ivanov on the church.

Prosecutor: You have said that if the church chooses someone else besides yourself, you would give him your place in the pulpit.

Kulichev: Yes. I would never impose myself.

Prosecutor: Then we are agreed. When will the election take place?

Kulichev: The end of the year is upon us. We'll have the election before the end of next January. First we must have the annual meeting of the church, and then the election for the office of pastor.

Prosecutor: Very good. But don't forget your responsibility under article 324 of the penal code.

Kulichev: This evening at 6 o'clock we are having a service in the church.

Prosecutor: And you will be the preacher?

Kulichev: Yes.

Prosecutor: In spite of everything we have just said?

Kulichev: Yes, in spite of everything. You know that there are many of us who are ready to sacrifice everything to do what is right.

Prosecutor: And in this way you hope for eternal life?

These words persuaded me that our conversation had made a deep impression on the prosecutor. There followed discussions with Cvetkov and representatives of the Ministry of Foreign Affairs.

Shortly after the new year began, the authorities apparently decided they had had enough of this insubordinate pastor who would not do as he was told. On January 9, 1985, they came to arrest me. But to my astonishment I was not charged with violating article 324 (exercising a profession without authorization) as I had expected, but rather article 274. This provision of the law makes it illegal to exercise the functions of a public official without authorization or after being relieved of the position; the maximum penalty was one year either in prison or in a forced labor camp.

The officers warned me that I would not be permitted to contact my family nor to receive food from them. I replied that it would be a problem not to receive food from the outside because I am a vegetarian. They answered that I could buy a half-kilogram [about one pound] of yellow cheese and 125 grams [two ounces] of butter and a packet of biscuits in the prison canteen each week so that nobody would think that my refusal of meat was due to a hunger strike. I requested that they call my wife with the news so she would not worry about my disappearance. But they replied that my brother Dimitar (who was the treasurer of the Congregational churches) would tell her; they had already alerted him about my arrest. They also mentioned that they had forgotten to tell Dimitar that if he did not cease his activities in the church, he would also end up behind bars.

So off to prison I went. Although the accused is not officially guilty before his trial, he is nevertheless deprived of his rights. One morning some of us were speaking in the dining hall, which is prohibited. The head jailer stopped in front of me and ordered me out of the room. I don't know if it is legal to deprive a prisoner of breakfast, but even if it isn't, there is no way for anyone to defend his rights. The prisoner who is only being investigated has his hair cut short like the other prisoners and is addressed as "citizen" rather than "comrade" as is the case with those on the outside. And he is deprived of all contact with those close to him.

After arriving at the prison I began a long series of interviews with my interrogator, a man named Penkov. These conversations were difficult because they did not follow the clear requirements of the law. Article 83 of the statutes says that the burden of proof is on the prosecutor and the authorities who conduct the investigation. In the same place the text clearly says that "the accused person is not obliged to prove that he is innocent." But Penkov told me frankly, "You will have to prove that you are not guilty."

These interrogations sometimes take months to complete. The interrogator is in no particular hurry, since time is on his side and the suspect is safely locked up. There is a kind of psychological terrorism in this process. The prisoner is expected to fret, to make demands, to stew in the juices of his impatience. But I had the conviction through it all that God was in control of the situation and not Penkov.

When Penkov finally called me in he wonderingly said, "You haven't asked me what is going on."

"What is there to ask you?" I replied. "I knew you would call when you needed me." During my forty days in the interrogation prison I met with him more than ten times, sometimes alone and sometimes with Dimitar, who had been jailed shortly after I was. From the beginning Penkov was astonished that I did not admit to having done anything illegal. I maintained that I was the ordained pastor of the church according to the church's own rules.

"But your rights as a pastor were taken away."

"That is not true. When and by whom were my rights taken away?"

"Haven't you admitted that Cvetkov met with you and your brother at the Committee for Religious Affairs and informed you fully?"

"That does not mean that I am deprived of my rights as pastor. I am pastor until the end of my life. It is only the college of pastors which can deprive me of this right if I fail to meet the requirements of the gospel for pastors. Show me the document which says that I am deprived of my rights as a pastor and that it is prohibited for me to preach. Even if such a document existed, that would not prove you are right. In our country, liberty of conscience and freedom of religion are guaranteed."

"Even if liberty of conscience and of religion are guaranteed, that does not mean you can act without obeying the law. We do not permit the church to be a state within the state. And we don't insert ourselves into its affairs. You have to understand that this is a secular society and that believers therefore make themselves the enemies of the state."

"In what way is the believer an enemy of the state? In that he is honest, that he does not betray anyone, nor lie, nor steal? In that he is faithful to his wife and has a healthy family? In that believers everywhere perform their duties conscientiously? Is that what makes them enemies of the state?"

"I am the one asking the questions here."

Our conversations sometimes led to our preaching to each other. I would explain the gospel of Jesus Christ to him, and he would declare what Marxist theory teaches about those issues, explanations which I had already heard many times. Penkov's real purpose seemed to be the same as that of Cvetkov and the prosecutor with whom I had talked: to get me to accept Ivanov's forced occupation of the pastorate. I responded that the identity of the pastor was a matter for the church to decide. If the church chose Ivanov, I would not object. But nobody could, in good conscience, accept the imposition of a pastor by force from the outside.

At our second meeting, Penkov informed me that my brother Dimitar had been arrested. I found out later that he was charged with having preached in the church one time. Penkov also told me that two men in the church had given in to the pressures placed upon them and no longer would object to Ivanov's occupation of the pulpit. And he added the news, the truth of which I could not ascertain, that Pavel Ivanov had already occupied the pulpit of the church. "Your comrades have abandoned you," he said. His strategy was to make me think I was all alone and thus weaken my resolve to continue to stand for the church's rights. He failed to see that I was looking to God for sustenance and strength and not to others.

We had many conversations on the matter of the missing document that I continually asked to see, the one that supposedly revoked my right to be a pastor. His answer was that the government had no responsibility to produce a document; the Committee had spoken and that was enough. But if the Committee is the supreme head of the church, then Jesus Christ has been replaced by an idol. This we could never accept. I put it to Penkov in these words: "You ask me to work in the church under your orders. Anyone who would consent to do that would not be serving God, but you." Responses like that would send Penkov into a threatening mood, sometimes promising me a prison term, other times psychiatric "treatment."

Penkov showed Dimitar and me the dossier he had established concerning the case and allowed us to read some of the documents (although he complained that we were studying them too thoroughly!). It was then that I understood how much turmoil had entered the life of the church. The two members who had agreed to the wishes of the state had done much damage. And Pavel Ivanov at one point had called in the police in order to be able to take possession of the pulpit, since a crowd of church members had physically blocked him. I was overwhelmed to read of the endurance and courage of the brothers and sisters in the church who continued their resistance to the takeover.

We knew before my arrest that the authorities had twice broken into the parsonage, which ordinarily houses the pastor of the church. Two officers of the Ministry of the Interior showed up there on the morning of January 3 with a locksmith. Cvetkov was also there, and he authorized them to open the door. But these efforts were frustrated because the other side of the door was blocked by thick planks nailed to the framing. The same was true of the other door to the house. Finally they broke down the door with an axe and installed Pavel Ivanov in the parsonage.

After forty days I was sent to the Kremikovci prison while Dimitar remained at the central prison. This move took place late in the evening of February 20. I had been at Kremikovci twenty years earlier when visiting a young Christian who had refused to report for military service. But the prison had grown so much larger in the interval that I did not recognize it.

One of the great blessings I had during this time was an illegal visit from my son. He brought with him clothing and food and also news, and he was also able to help some of those who were in the prison with me. During his third visit a fellow prisoner told me that this would be the last time it would be possible for him to come. I expressed my gratitude for even the few times he had been allowed into the prison. Some time later, on April 14, my family visited (for the first time officially) and again brought provisions. My wife packed in a separate container a piece of bread soaked in wine from a communion service. So I was able to celebrate the Lord's death and resurrection in common with other believers, joining myself spiritually with the great family of God.

Meanwhile, there was much optimism in the church when people had a chance to read the official complaint of the prosecutor. Everyone said there was nothing to the charges and that no tribunal would condemn us.

Dimitar and I were again together for the trial, having been transported in handcuffs to a windowless basement cell. The trial took place on April 23 and 24. On the 25th they read the verdict. We were surprised to see the small courtroom filled with people, with many more standing outside. It was not only our family who had come to wish us well, but more than a hundred people who had traveled from different parts of Bulgaria in order to encourage us by their presence.

Officials quickly ordered everyone out of the room; this was to be a trial conducted behind closed doors. There were arguments about this arrangement, but we later learned that the decision had been made beforehand; in fact, four days before the trial began, broadcasts to foreign countries had reported that the public would not be admitted. In a bizarre development, Cvetkov told those who waited outside the courtroom that the government had received two thousand letters of protest from foreign sources, but that this would make no difference. Everybody laughed when he said that we were going to be tried for *theft*. (Apparently there was some idea that they could pin on us charges of pilfering state materials from a construction site.) Later on he told others that we had been condemned for trading illegally in foreign exchange.

I thought from the start that we would be found guilty, that the court would not even consider the witnesses, the facts, and the documents that we could present. For if we were to be found innocent, it would be the same as declaring guilty those who brought us into court. And it would have recognized what we were claiming all along, that Pavel Ivanov had been imposed illegally on the church.

Cvetkov's testimony repeated the position of the Committee. But under cross-examination he made an admission that would have been damaging in a fair trial. Our lawyer asked if he knew that I had been pastor of the church at Krichim. Cvetkov replied that he knew I had preached there but that it was impossible that I could have been pastor, since that fact would have been registered in the Committee's records. The lawyer replied: "But there are documents that show he was indeed pastor there. Here, have a look at them." Cvetkov would not look at the papers the lawyer held out to him. Evidently he thought what we did: If I were already recognized officially as a pastor, then I could not be deprived of the right to be pastor of a church without another document which canceled that right. And that was the document he had always refused to produce.

The former pastor, Mr. Bojovaiski, testified that Pavel Ivanov could not have replaced him legally because his name had not been advanced as a candidate, either orally or in writing. To the lawyer's question about precedents to Ivanov's coming forward in the way he did, he replied there were none; nobody had ever come from Cvetkov claiming to be the pastor. He also said the church had never received anything in writing from the Committee to the effect that Dimitar and I had had our licenses revoked. There was only an oral message, and that had come from Cvetkov.

Pavel Ivanov testified, admitting that he had never been elected pastor by the church, but only by the Committee. Pressed by our lawyer, he acknowledged that he had entered the church and claimed the pulpit before he had a document authorizing him to do so; he acted thus only on the basis of an oral agreement with Cvetkov. Ivanov claimed that a number of people physically prevented him from taking the pulpit, but then admitted that Dimitar and I were not among them. Later in the trial someone testified that Ivanov had been expelled from another church for immorality.

Several people from the church recited the facts concerning Dimitar's and my ordination, the quality of our work, and the lack of anything against our moral standing. There was also unrefuted testimony that we never taught anything against the social order.

In their summation, the two defense lawyers went over the main facts that had come out of the trial, stressing that my election as pastor was done according to the rules of the church which were recognized by law, and that Pavel Ivanov's oral appointment by Cvetkov had no legal standing. He had usurped his position. There had been no evidence in the trial to refute these contentions.

The outcome was as we expected. The court found us guilty. Our family and lawyers expected that I would be given a sentence of six months and my brother four. But the actual sentences were eight months for me and six months for Dimitar, to be served in the Sopot prison.

We had many wonderful experiences in the prison. People were astonished to learn of the article under which we had been sentenced. Most of them didn't even know it existed. Both prisoners and jailers asked many questions, and it turned out that we had a more fruitful ministry there than we could have expected in church. God was better served by our presence in prison than if we had been free.

Such service is not confined to preaching in a pulpit or to occupying an important post, but to serve one's neighbor who is in trouble; to calm, encourage, and relieve a suffering soul; and to show him the way to eternal life.[2]

Notes

1. This chapter is taken from Pastor Kulichev's unpublished book, titled *Impressions from Prison.*

2. The following note was published by Keston College in *Frontier,* the issue of May-June 1989, p.25: "Bulgarian Congregational pastor Hristo Kulichev has finally been freed from his three-year term of exile. Kulichev, who was removed from his post as pastor of the Sofia church under pressure from the state, was given an exile sentence in April 1986. This was because he continued preaching after being removed from office. He has been back home in Sofia with his family for some time, receiving medical treatment, but it is only now that the authorities have fully lifted the remainder of his sentence."

EPILOGUE

O ne night in September 1989, Kent Hill, executive director of the Institute on Religion and Democracy in Washington, D.C., and Al Janssen, the editor of this book, left their hotel in Moscow to take a walk. As they passed by the Tchaikovsky Conservatory of Music, they noticed that a Baroque festival featuring a French quartet was scheduled to begin soon. They decided to buy tickets for the event and on approaching the ticket office they ran into Sergei Sevchenko, whom Hill had met earlier. Sevchenko exchanged his ticket so that the three of them could be seated together.

Sevchenko was a young physicist but spent his spare time with dissident Russian Orthodox people who were striving to reverse seventy years of Soviet repression of Christians. He was a close associate of Alexander Ogorodnikov, one of the best-known dissidents of the 1980s.

Fifteen months earlier, Ogorodnikov and I had spent a couple of days together during the unofficial International Civil Rights Congress in Moscow, noted among other things for its harassment by KGB goons. In his apartment one evening, Ogorodnikov told me of his conversion to Christ as a young philosophy student and of the heady days in the mid-1970s when he and some friends founded the Christian seminar in Moscow. The KGB had watched them closely for a time, but refrained from moving in until the group began issuing study papers, pounded out laboriously on a typewriter with multiple carbon copies. Then agents moved in and arrested the whole lot. Ogorodnikov held up before me a bound copy of the papers and said, "Eight-and-a-half years in a strict regime labor camp for this."

Now he was out, released by a general amnesty, and a number of serious-minded Christians like Sevchenko had joined him. Sevchenko was an accomplished photographer, and when Hill and Janssen met him, he was engaged in taking and assembling pictures which documented the destruction of churches by Communist authorities.

Here is Janssen's account of their evening:

We had a wonderful time. I remember being impressed with Sergei's strength of character. As I looked into his eyes, I saw a gentleness along with a steel resolve in a combination I've never quite seen in the West. We talked about our mutual faith, about his work as a photographer, about his love for music. He said he attended two or three concerts a week and found peace in his soul from the music. After the concert, Sergei walked back to our hotel with us and then continued on toward his home. He said it was his practice to walk for an hour or more after the concert. It was a time for meditation and reflection.

A month later Sergei Sevchenko was dead. On October 23, a car followed him as he left the concert hall on one of those meditative walks. It jumped the curb, sped along the sidewalk, and crushed the young physicist—the same method used by Romanian authorities as described by Peter Dugulescu in this book. Only eleven months earlier the KGB had silenced Ogorodnikov's brother, an Orthodox monk, in the same way.

During the short period between Sevchenko's death and the notification by the morgue of the whereabouts of his body, his entire collection of photographs of desecrated churches disappeared from his apartment. Probably not coincidental is the fact that his wife was out of town at the time, as was a close friend of his, the ambassador of the Netherlands.

Two weeks after the killing, Victor Grigoriev opened the door to the office of the *Bulletin of Christian Opinion,* a journal edited by Ogorodnikov and his friends, and was pounced upon by two strangers who quickly beat him into unconsciousness. When they left, three computers, two printers, a fax machine, and gifts from friends in the West had all vanished. It bore the hallmarks of another KGB operation.

Placed against these recent events, I recall other images that stand in sharp contrast. Only a week before I met Ogorodnikov, I watched Mikhail Gorbachev on a flickering black-and-white television screen, addressing the American people from the White House lawn. Russian friends with me in the small Leningrad apartment seemed bemused by the warm welcome the Soviet leader was receiving. And then, some eight months after Sevchenko's death, I was walking in a quiet Minneapolis neighborhood near my house when a large jet transport with four engines in the rear, trailing thick black smoke in a way I had not seen for twenty years or more, roared overhead. Gorbachev's airplane was bound for San Francisco. The people of Minnesota had just given him a hero's welcome.

How different was this attitude from that of the Soviet citizens I had spoken to earlier! They showed skepticism at best for the processes then taking place in their country. By the time Gorbachev came to Minnesota, that attitude had changed largely to distrust and open contempt.

No doubt much of the warmth for the Soviet leader in the United States and other western countries is due to relief at the ending of the cold war with its tensions and the worries about nuclear warfare. But there is also considerable wishful thinking about the man and the processes which led to the changes wrought under his direction. The collapse of the Soviet economy and the antagonism toward its ideology and practices in the minds of the Soviet people did not come about because Gorbachev and his colleagues are democrats. A false ideology has finally reached the end of its string and a brutal and illegitimate rule has begun to unravel, a process over which Gorbachev is presiding. Western euphoria is badly misplaced, as is adulation for the leader who presides over the collapse.

As the public will soon learn, a period of great uncertainty and danger approaches. We cannot know the future, but the fragmentation into national blocs of the once-monolithic Soviet state will bring dangers other than the kinds to which we have grown accustomed. The Moslem republics of the USSR will begin to exercise not only their repressed religion, but also their hatred of Christians, who have already begun to flee to other parts of the Soviet Union. As for the regime itself, the murder of Sevchenko—more than four years after the inauguration of *glasnost* and *perestroika*—should remind us that liberalization borne of desperation is not the same thing as genuine reform based on the desire for justice. We can hope and pray the latter will come, and in God's providence it may; but we must not imitate the media elite who speak as if the millennium has been ushered in by Soviet leaders.

I have written of the Soviet Union in this epilogue to illustrate a point that the Bible makes eloquently. "Remember the words I spoke to you: 'No servant is greater than his master.' If they persecuted me, they will persecute you also. If they obeyed my teaching, they will obey yours also" (John 15:20). Persecution is part of the normal Christian experience, a consequence of the desire to follow Christ with faithfulness. Those who do not go through it are part of the fortunate few. They should thank God for his mercy in this and seek to find ways to help those whose experience is closer to the norm.

The shifting prospect in the Soviet Union is not different in principle from that which takes place elsewhere. Persecution gets better or worse, perhaps disappears entirely for a time before reappearing. Its form changes. But the conditions that give rise to it, the unremitting enmity toward God and his people by those outside the Kingdom, do not change. That is why the complacency brought about by improving conditions is so badly placed. It encourages our blindness and helps mask from our eyes the realities of tyranny.

Before leaving Ogorodnikov's apartment I asked him what he and his friends hoped to accomplish by their activities. I thought he looked surprised as he answered, as if I should have known without asking. "We're trying to bring about Christian revival in the Soviet Union," he said slowly.

As long as that is the answer Christians give, there will be plenty of opposition. And the forms that it takes will often look something like the experiences related in this book.